BEGINNING READING INSTRUCTION IN DIFFERENT COUNTRIES

Lloyd O. Ollila, Editor
University of Victoria
Victoria, British Columbia
Canada

ira

Selected Papers, Part 1
Seventh IRA World Congress on Reading
Hamburg, August 1-3, 1978
Dorothy S. Strickland, Chairperson and Series Editor

International Reading Association
800 Barksdale Road
Newark, Delaware   United States of America

INTERNATIONAL READING ASSOCIATION

Copyright 1981 by the
International Reading Association, Inc.

Library of Congress Cataloging in Publication Data
World Congress on Reading, 7th, Hamburg, 1978.
  Beginning reading instruction in different countries.

  Selected Papers, Part 1, Seventh IRA World Congress on
Reading, Hamburg, August 1-3, 1978, Dorothy S. Strickland,
Chairperson and Series Editor.
  Includes bibliographies.
  1. Reading (Elementary)—Congresses. 2. Reading readi-
ness—Congresses   I. Ollila, Lloyd O.
II. Title.
LB1572.9.W67 1978   372.4'1   80-19294
ISBN 0-87207-428-5

Contents

ACKNOWLEDGMENTS

My thanks to the planning committee for IRA's Seventh World Congress on Reading and to all those who served as speakers and chairpersons and to those who participated as listeners and discussants. Only a small portion of the excellence displayed on that program is reflected in the published papers.

Much of the success of the Congress was due to IRA's extraordinary staff whose standards of excellence remained resolute in the face of lost luggage and the sometimes equally traumatic complexities of running a major convention.

My deep appreciation is extended to Faye R. Branca, IRA Professional Publications Editor, whose expertise and assistance in putting these volumes together proved invaluable.

DSS

Foreword

The International Reading Association, recognizing the importance of worldwide literacy, promotes international sharing of ideas through conferences and publications, as well as through the Unesco Literacy Award. *Beginning Reading Instruction in Different Countries*, edited by Lloyd Ollila, grew from papers presented at IRA's Hamburg World Congress. Dorothy S. Strickland, Chairperson of the Congress and President of IRA at the time the Congress was held in August 1978, serves as series editor for the three volumes developed from the papers presented in Hamburg.

Association members are well aware of the fundamental relevance of literacy to world peace and prosperity. They know that studying the problems and achievements of countries that have long sought the goal of universal literacy can help both developed and underdeveloped countries achieve much more than literacy. Here literacy is defined in a larger context than that of purely academic performance and is set within a framework of societal expectations and responsiblilites. These discussions illuminate many aspects of the role of beginning reading instruction in the multinational goals of literacy. The authors do more than help us understand other countries' reading programs; they provide a distillation of wisdom that reaches beyond mere information.

When asked why he was going to Paris for the eighth or ninth time, G.K. Chesterton replied that it would help him to see London more clearly. By looking through another's eyes at the problems and progress in beginning reading instruction, each of us can see our own work in a clearer light.

These authors describe approaches to beginning reading instruction in five different areas of the world, but they do not ask us to accept the "one right" approach. Far more temperate and wise, they search not for one best way, but for many ways, to benefit individual children. The authors describe numerous approaches to help teachers give human beings richer lives through literacy. These shared insights can guide the teacher who wonders which path to follow, although the present rich and varied increase in theory building and research fails to lead to a consensus. The probing and comprehensive reports from different countries allow us a perspective that could not be achieved by studying a single country. Comparative cross-national studies could help us see what is merely idiosyncratic (such as the age of school entrance) and what is essential (such as dealing with individual differences).

In some countries, the curriculum is mandated nationally; in others, the teacher is autonomous in determining it. Some educators rely heavily upon commercially prepared materials, others turn to child-made books and to children's literature. Reading and writing are taught incidentally and formally. There seems to be no one road to literacy; instead there are many paths to follow. There appears, however, to be general agreement about the importance of the roles of language acquisition and parental involvement in the reading process.

Reports from every country show that education in general and beginning reading instruction in particular attract national attention. While no other educators seem to "test" children as frequently as do Americans, there are national surveys and governmental committees assigned to investigate progress in many countries. It is evident that the nations reported in this volume take education seriously and recognize the fundamental role that reading plays. Clearly, each country is aware of the importance of seeking universal literacy for its immediate technological value as well as for its long distance cultural survival. And while many educators acknowledge that the various media serve very valuable functions, most teachers recognize that written literature best serves certain functions. Every culture realizes the necessity of seeking its own literature and that the goals of reading (literacy) are paramount.

Bernice E. Cullinan
New York University

Introduction

Giving children a successful, enjoyable introduction to reading is an important goal for all educators throughout the world. In the pages that follow, writers describe, report trends, and discuss various unique aspects of beginning reading programs in Sweden, Japan, North America, England, and Mexico.

Eve Malmquist reports on beginning reading in Sweden. In this country, as in other Scandinavian countries, children are introduced to reading instruction at age seven. The writer discusses various principles of instruction and methods used at this time. He points out trends in approaching beginning reading instruction including the teaching of immigrant children. He stresses the importance of a verbal environment, teacher competence, and early diagnosis in reducing reading disabilities.

In the second article Takahiko Sakamoto discusses the various methods and materials used to introduce Japanese preschoolers to reading. He reports that children begin reading prior to school in an informal setting with the help of their parents, especially the mother. Many Japanese children start learning Hiragana (a Japanese writing system) at four years of age. Sakamoto describes recent research on the teaching of Kanji (a more difficult writing system). Finally he describes recent trends of research on beginning reading in Japan.

Beginning reading in North America is described by Lloyd Ollila and Joanne Nurss, first from a historical perspective and then from a report on current practices and trends. Such practices as developing reading readiness and rationales for beginning reading at age six can be better understood in a historical light. The authors report on various methods, materials and instructional organizations used to prepare children and to begin formal reading instruction in kindergarten and grade one.

Vera Southgate describes beginning reading in England. She begins by acquainting the reader with three features of the English education system: the autonomy of the head teacher, the flexibility of the English education system, and the length of infant education. Then the organization and reading schemes used in infant classes are described. How a teacher introduces English children to reading and the importance of the Infant Reading Scheme are reported. Current philosophies, developments, future trends, and the author's personal viewpoint are discussed in the light of developments over the past twenty-five years in English education.

Finally, Robert Miller discusses basic reading in Mexico. At the beginning of his chapter he incorporates a brief preview of the administration of Mexican schools to provide a content for his description of beginning reading instruction. He then details the official method of reading instruction, the "metodo global de analisis," and shows how it is applied from grade one through grade six.

This book is dedicated to teachers around the world. May you continue to enrich and bring new meaning and joy to the lives of children.

Lloyd O. Ollila

Beginning Reading in Sweden

Eve Malmquist
University of Linköping
Linköping, Sweden

Age of School Entrance and Beginning Reading

We know very little about the considerations behind the choice of age of school entrance in different countries. In most cases, these decisions were made a long time ago. Most children in the United States and Canada enter school at six years of age and the assumption is that they all will be taught to read in the first grade. At least that is the general expectation of the children and their parents.

In countries such as West Germany, Hungary and France (to mention only a few), the general practice also is to start the teaching of reading at the age of six. But the age at which the majority of children are introduced to reading varies from country to country. For example, in Great Britain, New Zealand, and Australia formal reading instruction begins at age five. Schools in the Scandinavian countries—Denmark, Finland, Norway, and Sweden—and also those in Poland and the Soviet Union do not introduce reading instruction until age seven, and sometimes even later, depending upon the maturational level of the individual child. At present, there is a tendency in many countries to reconsider the regulations concerning the age at which a child is allowed to enter school.

In the process of reconsideration, the results of comparative cross-national studies should be of great value. My bold introductory statement in this respect is that all nations having stipulated a certain age of school entrance are wrong—

1

regardless of whether this age is five, six, seven, or any other age.

Children of the same chronological age differ widely in their capacity to learn, their intelligence, their background experiences, and in all kinds of personality traits. Research workers all over the world are in agreement on this point. My own investigations of first grade children in Sweden (4) uncovered a range in mental age from 4 years and 11 months to 11 years and 8 months, while differences between the children's chronological ages were very small (7 years ± 3 months).

A great range of ability as to other variables at school entrance was also noted in another experimental study in Sweden. The writer found a number of seven year old first grade children in the population studied who did not know even the letters in their own names. Only 2 to 3 percent of these children knew all the small letters; 80 percent of them could not read a single word in an easy prose text, standardized for the end of the spring term of the first grade. On the other hand, around 2 percent of the children were able to read at an achievement level equivalent to that of the beginning of third grade.

Taking into account the observed great differences as to maturation and abilities in various respects between children of the same age, I am of the opinion that the use of a fixed chronological age as a criterion of a child's readiness for school entry and learning to read should be opposed regardless of whether a country has chosen five, six, or (as Sweden) seven years of age as the delimiting factor for school entry. It seems to me that a flexible time for starting school and a slow and successive introduction of pupils from the preschool to the school is the only reasonable administrative policy to be recommended. An integration of preschool and primary school would de-emphasize the school start and make it function better and more naturally.

School Maturity and Reading Readiness

I share the opinion of the Swedish school authorities that, for personality development and mental health of children, it is extremely important that their contact with school be positive from the very beginning. Children should be given opportunities to feel the great satisfaction and motivation for continued work that is connected with success in learning to read and write.

But I believe that the age factor has been overestimated as a criterion of school maturity in Sweden, as well as in most other countries, and I feel greater flexibility as to beginning age in Swedish schools is highly desirable.

The concepts of school maturity and reading readiness should be looked upon as relative and not as absolute. Concepts of this kind should be considered in terms of learning and adjustments of various kinds that the first year curriculum demands of beginners—and, even more, the adjustments the school is prepared to make to the prerequisites of the children.

There is obviously a great need for more research on a cross-national scale before any more general conclusions can be made concerning the optimum age for the introduction of formal reading instruction to the majority of children in a given cultural area. Further, a great number of factors other than chronological age are to be considered when we try to determine the best age for beginning reading—factors such as the developmental level of the child, the number of pupils in the class, the competence and the experience of the teachers, the nature of the instructional material, and the teaching methods. Teaching a four or five year old child to read in a one teacher-one pupil relationship is, of course, quite different from a situation where you have one teacher and twenty-five to thirty-five pupils.

Many years ago, Jack Holmes made a statement in this connection which still seems to me to be of interest. He linked the ability of young children to the pupil-teacher ratio. "Other things being equal, the earliest stage at which a child can be taught to read is a function of the amount of time or help the teacher can give the pupil" (1). The younger the child, the more individual care and instruction is necessary. After having done a summary of available research within this area, Holmes came to the conclusion that the class size should be fewer than ten children if the teaching of reading to children below the age of five is to have any chance of success.

The Critical First Stages of Learning to Read
Inappropriate Techniques Difficult to Unlearn

A failure in the early stages of learning to read may negatively affect a child's entire personality development. This view is becoming more widely accepted by both Swedish school authorities and by teachers.

Good habits are critical in the acquisition of any new skill. Repetition is good only if what is being repeated is appropriate and desirable; otherwise, it can be very harmful. Inappropriate attitudes (for instance, toward reading), as well as inappropriate techniques, can be extremely difficult to unlearn. The first stages of learning to read are, therefore, considered to be of critical importance.

In Sweden it is held that growth in reading, as growth in other learnings, cannot be hurried without some undesirable, even damaging, effects. Therefore, we try to make the transition from home to school as easy as possible by having the children go to school for only two hours a day the first two or three weeks of school, and in groups of no more than twelve or thirteen children. Even if the majority of seven year old children are ready to be taught reading when they start school, there are always some who, for various reasons, have not reached the desired readiness level. It is considered unrealistic to expect these children to make normal progress in reading. Whatever the reasons for their lack of readiness, the school must let them get a calm and cautious start in reading and stimulate their development toward reading readiness in all possible ways *before* formal instruction in reading starts. Otherwise, these children run a big risk of becoming "failures" and of developing a lifelong dislike of reading.

Organizational Steps Furthering Individualization

According to the objectives stated in the Swedish school law, the school has to stimulate children's personal growth toward development as free, self-active, self-confident, and harmonious human beings. The school must give individual education.

The need for organizing instruction to adequately provide for individual differences between and within children as to various capacities, background experiences, and personality traits, is found to be more evident and urgent. Much still remains to be done in practical application before the proud and far-reaching declarations in the school law are even near realization.

Some few steps have been taken to further a diagnostic approach and individualization in teaching reading. Class size has been reduced to a maximum of twenty-five pupils in the three first years and to thirty in the remaining six years of compulsory schooling. (Presently the mean size, for the country as a whole, lies between seventeen and eighteen pupils per class.) A further reduction of class size is being discussed.

The teacher is allowed to divide the class into two groups and teach only one group at a time for ten hours out of the children's weekly schedule of twenty hours in the first grade. By this means, the teacher has no more than thirteen students at a time, often no more than eight to ten. This procedure has significantly contributed to giving teachers better opportunities for individualized teaching.

Some improvements have been noted as to the opportunities for individual tutoring, group teaching, and remedial teaching of reading in clinics and in ordinary classes. A bill accepted by the Swedish Parliament, and in effect since July 1, 1978, will increase the possibilities for a flexible use of personnel and financial resources at local municipality and individual school levels. Governmental subsidies to individual municipalities may now be used the way the local school authorities find most reasonable and efficient in actual situations.

Special teachers may be used for individual tutoring of children with reading difficulties, for remedial teaching in reading clinics or remedial reading classes or, if more desirable, as counselors and active assistants to regular teachers in direct teaching in classrooms. Teams of teachers of parallel classes may be formed.

Local schools may adjust financial and personnel resources to actual needs more so than before. Such a decentralization of the power of decision making as to the best use of teacher resources is a step in the right direction for improvement of the treatment and teaching of low achievers in the

Swedish schools. It is important to help children with reading disabilities and, ideally, to prevent reading disabilities from arising through early diagnosis and effective treatment. I do not believe, however, that there is enough stress on the necessity of also devoting special attention and care to the good readers—the high achievers.

Here the rigid age-graded school system in Sweden has another weak point. The common attitude that high achievers (good readers) will get along under all circumstances is, from my point of view, a very dangerous one. No nation can afford to waste its talents, but that is what happens if the most talented, the most gifted pupils in a class are insufficiently motivated to strive toward higher levels of reading skills. In Sweden, gifted children are very often kept at the pace of the average readers in the class. From my point of view, high achievers in the Swedish primary schools should be given much more demanding reading tasks than is now the case. They should be more steadily challenged to raise their levels of reading performance.

No Reading Instruction in the Preschool

A firmly established tradition in Sweden implies that children should not receive reading instruction in the pre-school. In the same way, parents avoid teaching their children to read at preschool age. They answer children's questions as to words and letters, but very seldom enter into a real teaching situation. They are afraid of doing something wrong. A child will learn to read from a professional teacher in the primary school. That's the accepted principle. We have not yet found a satisfactory answer to the question: "Why should we teach reading to two, three, or four year old children?" This may be possible, but we ask: "Is it advisable?" "Is it desirable?" "At what price?"

This philosophy seems to be quite in contrast to the view held by some people (for example, in the United States of America) that we ought to lower the beginning age and push children to achieve reading ability at a more accelerated speed than hitherto. The truth may lie somewhere between these extremes. In my country, we may have gone too far in our ambition to diminish the risk of failures by using much time in overlearning reading readiness skills.

There are evident and unfortunate barriers between preschools and primary schools in Sweden. For a number of years, I have urged that we consider the teaching of reading as a continuous developmental process, ongoing from early childhood to adulthood. As a consequence of this theory, a closer cooperation (even a real connection) between preschool and first grade in school should be established, and a greater flexibility as to the age of beginning reading could be applied.

Verbal Environment in the Early Years

There is in Sweden (as in many other countries) enough evidence to give us reason to state that children's progress in learning to read is, to a considerable extent, dependent upon their experiences with the use of the spoken word in their preschool years. Thinking and language develop simultaneously.

The extension of meaning in language is a lifetime process. But lack of adequate training in the early years of life may seriously hamper the development of later reading performance—indeed, personality development as a whole.

Children living in homes on a low cultural level, where the adults are speaking a poor language characterized by a great paucity of ideas and thoughts, will be greatly handicapped. Poor verbal environments, where adults seldom speak to children and conversation is limited in extent and variety, will negatively influence children's development of speaking ability and cause great reading problems later.

Children who grow up in environments where there are books available, much reading is done, and books are treated with respect, have better prospects of becoming good readers. Poor readers tend to come from homes which have a lower standard of general culture than the homes of good readers. The development of reading ability is considered to reflect not only inherent aptitude but also opportunities for adequate training and motivation for learning (2, 3, 4). For most children, learning to read is their first encounter with a type of learning involving abstract symbols intended to be associated with previous experiences. If children have not been given opportunities to acquire backgrounds of meaningful concepts, and if the words presented in print are not a part of their speaking vocabularies and used with adequate understanding, children most likely will be greatly handicapped in their reading efforts from the very beginning.

The Objectives Decide the Procedures, Methods, and Materials to Be Used

In order to be able to choose good procedures for teaching, teachers must be quite clear about the objectives of their reading instruction. It is generally recognized that the first goal of reading instruction is to develop the mechanics of reading skill. Words may be identified by sight, by the use of context, or by structural analysis. The skill of oral reading with good expression, pitch, and enunciation should also be included.

Meaning Is Stressed from the Very Beginning

From the very beginning of reading instruction, teachers must stress various comprehension aspects. If reading is to be developed to act as a tool of learning, and if we want children to learn to like reading (the most important goal of all here roughly mentioned), the children must feel from the very beginning the meaning of what is taught during the reading lessons.

Methods of Instruction

Research in Sweden and elsewhere has shown that no one method of teaching reading is best for all children. Rather, teachers should look for some proper combination of methods best fitted for each child. More research is needed, however, in order to identify procedures for teachers to match appropriate methods to the aptitudes, skills, attitudes, and interests of each child.

In Sweden you will find two main groups of methods used for the teaching of reading—analytic and synthetic. But none exists in a pure form. All the existing basal reader systems use both analytic and synthetic methods, although in different proportions. Lately some alternative methods for learning to read (for instance, the language experience approach and psycholinguistic methods of various kinds) have caught the attention of Swedish teachers. They are mostly used as supplements to the traditional methods. With reference to the wide range of developmental ages in the school classes, it is held that every program of teaching reading should contain both synthetic and analytic methods from the very beginning. Otherwise, there could be no provision for the aim that every individual should be given special assistance as needed.

In short, the exclusive use of only one method would not be approved of in Sweden. In the United States, most reading specialists seem to have a similar view. The essential difference seems to lie in the timing of the various methods of acquiring elementary reading skills. We combine synthetic and analytic methods from the very beginning.

In the United States, the methods are mostly used in one or another kind of sequence. In Sweden, as well as in Belgium and Denmark, all phases of the language arts—namely listening, speaking, writing, and reading—are integrated from the first lesson of formal reading instruction. In the United States, on the other hand, writing is usually introduced at some later point in the program.

Writing of words, syllables, and letters is taught in Sweden from the very first lessons in the formal teaching of reading. Writing is supposed to support the teaching of reading. We prefer to use manuscript writing to cursive writing in these earlier stages, as the manuscript letters are more like the printed ones than are the cursive letters. They are easier to read and easier for the children to write with their immature motor ability at this developmental level.

The trend in Sweden is for combined methods to be used, mostly side by side from the very first reading lessons. Whole word attack and sentence attack are used as well as an attack of words by synthesizing the various letters in the word by "sounding." Still, the phonics method is the predominant basic teaching procedure for the majority of the teachers. The question to be answered is not "Should phonics be used?" but, rather, "When?" "To what extent?" and "With whom?"

Teacher Competence Dynamic Rather than Static

All good teachers do not behave in the same way. This means that effective teachers may achieve their excellent results in different ways. In Sweden, we no longer speak of teacher competence (teacher effectiveness) as one single trait of a uniform character. We prefer to think of teacher effectiveness as a multidimensional and complex trait. Good teachers are in command of many competencies. They are able to adjust their behaviors (methods of teaching) to the purpose of learning and to the varied background skills and knowledge of different pupils. They should also be able and willing to continue learning from their own and/or their colleagues' experiences, as well as from well documented research results.

We like to view teacher competence as dynamic rather than static. Good teachers find it more productive to search for appropriate methods and procedures compatible with specific learners, environments, and learning tasks rather than to search for the single best or most popular method and procedure.

Surprisingly, teacher competence has not been found to be a very important factor in beginning reading. Significant relationships were noted in extensive first grade studies in Sweden between the teacher's number of years of service and pupil achievement in reading. In our research (6, 7), we have found that teachers with more than six years of service attain better results in reading than teachers with less than six years.

Teaching of Immigrant Children

When discussing literacy and beginning reading, we must not forget to consider the great change in the educational situation which has taken place in Sweden during the past few decades due to the literacy needs of the immigrants. Taking into account both foreign residents in the country, naturalized immigrants, and children of immigrants, some 10 percent of the total population in Sweden is of foreign origin. According to official statistics, immigration accounts for 43 percent of the total rise in the Swedish population during 1944-1975. In 1970, special guidelines for the teaching of immigrant children were included in the curriculum for the elementary school. It has been stated that the aim of the education for immigrant children should be active bilingualism.

In a bill adopted by the Swedish Parliament in 1976 and which has come into effect from the autumn term 1977, the following program was put forward (8):

1. All children attending nursery school and day nursery, elementary school and upper secondary school, and speaking or regularly hearing a foreign language in their homes are to be entitled to home language lessons and practice.
2. It will be the duty of municipal authorities to inform immigrant children and their parents of home language practice and teaching facilities.
3. Grants-in-aid will be paid to municipalities to help cover the cost of home language instruction.
4. Priority is to be given to preschool education and the junior and middle levels of elementary school, since the children's linguistic and personal development is dependent on their being given an early opportunity of developing their first language (home language) in order to be able to be actively bilingual.

Some Research Results on Beginning Reading

It may be appropriate to mention also a few Swedish research studies having bearing on the teaching of beginning reading even if it must be done in a very condensed form.

Factors Related to Reading Disabilities in the First Grade

Some years ago I carried out rather extensive investigations on factors related to reading disabilities in the first grade of the comprehensive school. More than forty variables were studied in their relation to reading ability. Attention was paid to children's preschool development (birth, health, speech development). The children's (social and economic status), the educational level of their parents, and other environmental factors were taken into consideration. Moreover, the respective teachers evaluated a number of personality factors for each pupil: vision, hearing, reading ability, visual perception, spelling ability, and intelligence were tested. Some teacher and school variables were included in the studies.

The following factors were found to be most closely related to reading disabilities in the first grade and also were the factors that most distinctly differentiated the group of poor readers from the group of good readers: intelligence, ability to concentrate, persistence, self-confidence, and emotional stability; ability to spell according to some spelling tests and visual perception measured by five visual perception tests; socioeconomic group, parents' level of education, and interest in reading in the home; experience of children's teachers, measured by number of years in the profession.

On the basis of detailed case studies, it was found that children with special reading disabilities (the concept operationally defined) deviated very markedly from the mean of the population studied with respect to several other variables in addition to reading ability. To judge by these results, reading disabilities at first grade level are never isolated defects. In all the cases studied, reading disabilities existed together with deficiencies, disturbances, or unfavorable conditions in many other areas.

Judging by the results of these investigations, it appears reasonable to conclude that to attempt to find a single factor which will entirely explain the occurrence of reading disabilities is, in the majority of cases, a vain endeavor. There appear to be several factors in constellation which frequently are related to reading failure. Many of these factors seem to be closely interrelated. There appears to be an interplay between children's general physical, intellectual, emotional, and social development and the development of their reading abilities. For a broader discussion, see Malmquist and Valtin (7) and Malmquist (4).

Reduction of Cases of Reading Disabilities

The number of cases of reading disabilities in grades one through three of the comprehensive school may be considerably reduced by an early, careful diagnosis of all children starting in grade one and by the immediate establishment of a teaching situation synthesizing ongoing diagnosis, treatment, and remedial teaching for those children who, on the basis of the diagnostic findings, could be expected to experience special reading disabilities when offered only ordinary teaching facilities.

By the use of specially constructed test batteries, it is possible to put forward a much more reliable prediction than before regarding the development of the children's reading ability. Test use would also decrease to a considerable extent the error margin in the selection of pupils needing remedial teaching in a reading clinic.

A six year longitudinal study was conducted in twelve cities in Sweden. The investigation comprised a pilot study of twenty classes with a total of 386 pupils and a field study of seventy-two classes with a total of 1,653 pupils. Using an operational definition of special reading disabilities, it was found that 83 percent of the cases identified as potential reading disability cases were prevented from occurring. It was originally hoped that it would be possible to eliminate reading disability cases through remedial procedures such as those used with the experimental group in this research project. Unfortunately, this hope was not realized (3, 4).

Teaching Reading in Preschool

During a four year longitudinal project, the effect of individualized reading and writing instruction for six year olds at preschool was studied as compared with ordinary preschool activities, not including reading and writing instruction. This effect was studied with reference to the development of the pupils' reading and writing skills up to the end of grade three of the comprehensive school (5).

This is the very first systematic investigation carried out in Sweden which included the teaching of reading and writing to six year old children. The results of the investigation show that with early identification of potential reading failures, conscientious follow up of language development, and cautious individualized teaching of reading and writing at a low speed, the number of pupils needing special remedial reading in reading clinics and remedial reading classes was greatly diminished during the first three years in the comprehensive school (around 45 percent reduction).

The early start in learning to read and write was found to be of special importance for verbally handicapped children coming from environments where the adults seldom speak to the children and conversations are limited in extent and variety. The slow speed in the preschool training gave them fair opportunities to succeed in acquiring the necessary background of meaningful concepts, a sufficiently large vocabulary, and the abilities to listen attentively and to speak reasonably well.

The experimental group children were superior to the control group children at practically all intelligence and maturity levels at the end of first grade. The effects of the early training in reading and writing, according to the model used, were found to remain through grades two and three, although the differences between the test results of the two groups were getting smaller.

The main conclusion I have drawn from this experiment is that, for various reasons, verbally handicapped children profit by early identification and assistance and a prolonged time for learning the basic skills in reading and writing (four years instead of three for the attainment of the same general objectives).

Concluding Remarks

The overview of primary reading practices in a number of countries gives one reason to state that our knowledge of the various aspects of beginning reading skill is rather limited. There is a great need for cross-national comparative studies of the initial stages of learning to read, focusing on the effectiveness of different methods of teaching related to the characteristics of languages and to different ages at entering school.

The age of school entrance, for instance, and its implications for achievement are not readily studied within countries, so the cross-national comparison would lead to a better assessment of this factor. It is not only a question of which entrance age produces the highest reading attainment at the age of, let us say, nine years but also a question of possible differences as to the learning sequence among groups of children who start learning to read at different ages.

Considerations of a varied set of linguistic differences could lead to clearer insights regarding how best to arrange materials for beginning readers in accordance with the old didactic principle—from the easier to the more difficult.

Should children be kept in preschool longer and the start of reading instruction consequently be delayed? Or should children leave their preschool environment earlier and enter school earlier? Once in school, should they be taught to read immediately? These and similar questions are asked in many countries and the availability of cross-national data concerning these problems may well make it possible to reach more conclusive answers and contribute to a better basis for decision making with regard to some vital issues of primary reading.

References

1. HOLMES, JACK. "When Should and Could Jonny Learn to Read?" in J.A. Figurel (Ed.), *Challenge and Experiment in Reading*, proceedings of the Seventh Annual Convention of the International Reading Association. New York: Scholastic Magazines, 1962, 237-241.
2. MALMQUIST, EVE. *Factors Related to Reading Disabilities in the First Grade of the Elementary School.* Stockholm, Sweden: 1958.
3. MALMQUIST, EVE. *Lässvårigheter på grundskolans lågstadium. Experimentella studier. (Reading Disabilities at the Primary Stage, Experimental Studies,* with a summary in English.) Research Report No. 13 from the National School for Educational Research. Falköping, Sweden: 1969.
4. MALMQUIST, EVE. *Läs- och skrivsvårigheter hos barn. Analys och behandlingsmetodik. (Reading and Writing Disabilities in Children.)* Lund, Sweden: 1977.
5. MALMQUIST, EVE. *The Effects of Individualized Teaching of Reading and Writing to Preschool Children,* stencil, Linköping University, 1978.
6. MALMQUIST, EVE, and ANDRÉ INIZAN. *Les Difficultés d'apprendre à lire.* Paris: 1973.
7. MALMQUIST, EVE, and RENATE VALTIN. *Förderung Legastenischer Kinder in der Schule.* West Germany: Weinheim and Basel, 1974.
8. SWEDISH MINISTRY OF EDUCATION. Ministry of Education, Ministry of Labour, Swedish National Commission for Unesco. Meeting of specialists on the literacy needs of migrants, Stockholm, 1977.

Beginning Reading in Japan

Takahiko Sakamoto
Noma Institute of Educational Research
Tokyo, Japan

Reading of Hiragana

Hiragana, which is one of the three writing systems used in Japan, is a set of phonetic symbols. Each symbol in the Hiragana system is monosyllabic without any meaning by itself. With few exceptions, each symbol has only one phonetic pronunciation. Since the relationship between written symbols and spoken syllables is so very regular, the learning of Hiragana is not difficult. The number of basic symbols in Hiragana is 46. With the 46 symbols, plus other marks that give additional phonetic values, we can make up a total of 71 Hiragana letters, with which we can write any word or any sentence in the language.

Japanese children enter elementary school at age six, at which time the Ministry of Education requires that they start to learn the Hiragana letters. However, many children begin to learn Hiragana before school age without receiving any formal instructions, naturally absorbing Hiragana in their daily life through books, magazines, toys, TV programs, and the help of their family.

According to a nationwide research survey on reading and writing ability in preschool children, The National Language Research Institute of Japan (7) reports the following:

Adapted from Takahiko Sakamoto, "Beginning Reading in Japan," in Derek Thackray (Ed.), *Growth in Reading*. Published by the United Kingdom Reading Association, England. Reprinted with permission.

1. Many preschool children in Japan begin to learn Hiragana at the age of four.
2. When the test was given to four year old children who were still seventeen months away from entering elementary school, those who could not read any of the 71 Hiragana letters at all were only 9 percent of all the surveyed children, while 53 percent of them could read more than 21 letters, and 34 percent more than 60.
3. When the test was given to five year old children who were due to enter elementary school in five months, only 1 percent of all the investigated children could not read any of the Hiragana letters, while 82 percent of them could read more than 21 and 64 percent of them could read more than 60.
4. In the city areas, 88 percent of preschool children could read more than 60 Hiragana letters one month before entering elementary school.
5. Girls read better than boys.
6. There was one child with an exceptionally high reading ability who could read not only all the Hiragana letters but also 566 Kanji characters before entering school.

From these findings, we can see that Japanese children start learning Hiragana at about four years of age and that their reading abilities are considerably developed before entering elementary school.

This survey also reported that the level of children's reading abilities in 1967 was higher than that of 1953. In 1953, when the children were tested in the first month of their elementary school life, they averaged 26.2 basic Hiragana symbols read out of the basic 46. In 1967, however, five year old children who were tested five months before entering school read 36.8, and even the four year old children who were tested seventeen months before entering school read an average of 24.4 Hiragana out of the 46 symbols. That is, the four year olds in 1967 could read approximately as many Hiragana as could the first graders in 1953.

It is believed that parents' concern about the reading of their children is one of the most important factors in preschool children's reading. Recently, mothers' concern has increased greatly owing to the wider recognition of the importance of mental development during preschool age.

Parents, however, do not actually teach children to read letters. According to the report of the nationwide survey mentioned previously, to the question " How did your child learn to read?" those parents who reported that they themselves taught their children were less than 20 percent of all the surveyed parents, 2094 in number. The majority of the parents reported that they usually gave the children picture books, gave them Hiragana blocks (which were bought by about 70 percent of the parents), read books to them, and answered their children's questions about letters, all of which were more important than teaching them letters in a lesson-like situation.

Although letters or characters are formally taught in fewer than 20 percent of all Japanese kindergartens, a great amount of written Hiragana can be seen in most kindergartens, and children's questions about letters are answered by practically all teachers. We might say that the usual steps in teaching preschool children to read Hiragana at home and at kindergarten are first to give children numerous chances to see Hiragana at an early stage to arouse their interest in letters, and then to answer the children's questions about letters.

Japanese children are thought to be ready to learn to read Hiragana letters when they can divide the spoken language into constituent ON. The smallest unit of the Japanese language, ON means sound. Briefly speaking, an ON is a vowel or a combination of a consonant and a vowel. Each ON sound is written using one Hiragana letter. My name, Sakamoto, for example, has four sounds so it is written in four Hiragana letters (SA-KA-MO-TO). When children can divide spoken words into sounds, they are considered to be ready to start to learn to read.

Reading of Kanji

Kanji characters are ideographs that originally came from China. They are, therefore, often called Chinese characters from a literal translation of the term into English. Kanji, however, are no longer strictly Chinese; today they are very typically Japanese. They are read differently and the significance of some characters in Japan is entirely different from that of the Chinese. Because they are ideographs, each Kanji has its own meaning, and they are therefore quite numerous. Presently, however, they are officially limited to 1850 characters for daily use. The learning of Kanji is more difficult than the learning of Hiragana, not only because Kanji are more numerous but also because, unlike Hiragana, each Kanji usually has several alternative readings that range from monosyllabic to quadrasyllabic sounds. The Ministry of Education presently requires that 996 Kanji characters be learned during the six years of elementary school and 854 during the three years of junior high school, so that children complete the learning of all 1850 Kanji for daily use in the nine years of their compulsory education. Thus, children come to be able to read standard Japanese sentences in which there is a combination of Kanji and Hiragana, where 25 to 35 percent of the total number of characters is written in Kanji and the rest in Hiragana.

It has long been believed that children do not begin to learn Kanji unless they have completed the learning of Hiragana and that Kanji is, therefore, difficult for preschool children. There is, however, some evidence which contradicts this belief. Sakamoto (2) reported that of the 317 five year old kindergarten pupils surveyed only 14 percent could not read any of the tested 32 Kanji characters five months before entering elementary school. The rest of the children (86 percent) could read at least one Kanji. An average child could read six Kanji and over 17 percent of all the children could read no less that one-half of the tested 32 Kanji. It is certain that these children learned this amount of Kanji without formal instruction since Kanji had never been taught at the kindergarten where the survey was conducted.

I. Ishii, an experienced elementary school teacher of Kanji, began the experimental teaching of Kanji at a number of kindergartens in 1968. According to his research, the most suitable age for children to start learning Kanji is three years old. Ishii says an average child can learn more than 500 Kanji and a brighter child can learn about 1000 Kanji before school age, if the child is taught properly at age three. One of the main principles of the so-called Ishii program is to arouse children's curiosity or interest in Kanji. Ishii suggests that kindergarten teachers not hesitate to present Kanji to children even when they cannot read at all. Another principle of the Ishii program is repetition. Children must study a certain Kanji over and over again. Although the Ishii program is rather intensive and hard to follow perfectly, it has been accepted by more than 200 kindergartens since 1968.

The results of all subsequent experimental studies have, without exception, agreed with Ishii, at least in that the children who were taught at kindergarten could read much more Kanji than those who were not taught at all. Sakamoto (2) also reported that the experimental group of five year old children, who had been taught about 150 Kanji over the course of the previous year at kindergarten, could read an average of 50 Kanji characters ten months before entering elementary school, while the control group children of the same age, who were not taught any Kanji at all, could read an average of only 5 characters. Although they admit the efficacy of teaching Kanji at this stage, many researchers as well as educators who are interested in preschool reading are not necessarily positive in their assessment of the Ishii program. They worry whether too much emphasis on this sort of intellectual activity at the preschool stage might not distort the sound development of the child as a whole. Further investigation and consideration are needed in regard to the problem of teaching Kanji to preschool children.

Publications for Preschool Children

Shuppan Nenkan, The Publication Yearbook, Shuppan Nenkan Henshu Bu (4), published in Tokyo, reported that more than 300 new titles of books and 40 different magazines for preschool children were published in Japan in 1975. These books are usually called picture books because they contain mainly pictures with only a limited quantity of words or letters. Recently, however, picture books which emphasize letters or stories have been published and have been selling well. The majority of picture books published in Japan are what we call "story picture books" with rather long stories. Some of them are original Japanese works while others are Japanese versions of foreign classics. Many of the foreign classics are not only translated into Japanese but also rewritten for preschool children. It would be better, perhaps, to call them Japanese preschool versions of foreign classics. There are quite a few of them: *Heidi, The Little Princess, Little Lord Fauntleroy, Gulliver's Travels*, and the like. Although some people are against this kind of preschool version, claiming that it spoils the beauty of the original work, these versions are widely accepted by parents because of what they think is the importance of letting young children experience joy through books. Besides story picture books, there are in Japan what we call "animal picture books," "vehicle picture books," "daily life picture books," "knowledge picture books," "monster picture books," and "TV picture books." Preschool children are also very fond of magazines written expressly for them, and the most popular title sells more than a million copies a year.

All these books and magazines are printed in Hiragana only, which enables them to be read by many preschool children.

Recent Trends of Research on Beginning Reading

No research on preschool children's ability to read has been done in the past ten years because this topic is no longer appealing to Japanese researchers. Instead, researchers have started to investigate 1) what parents do and should do about their children's reading, 2) how children react to books, and 3) what makes picture books interesting. Here are some examples of recent research reports.

Sugiyama and Saito (5) reported that 36 percent of the surveyed preschool children's parents in Niigata prefecture, usually mothers, began to read books to their children when the children were one year of age, 31 percent of them began when the children were two years old, and 23 percent of them at the age of three. Only 7 percent of the parents had not read to their children until they were four years of age. This report also concluded that the earlier the parents began to read to their children, the more fluently the children could read by themselves when they were five years of age. To the extent that the mother's concern for the reading of her child is insufficient, the child's reading development is delayed.

Izumoji and others (1) reported that 92 percent of the preschool children they surveyed had picture books read to them at home. Mothers were the ones most often cited as the person who read picture books to their children, followed by both parents, and elder siblings. Fathers alone rarely read to them. Mothers answered that they gave picture books to their children because they wanted to let children know the joy of reading and to foster their interest in reading. Twenty percent of the mothers gave the first picture book to their children when the child was less than one year old, 50 percent when the child was one year old, 21 percent when two years old, 6 percent when three years old, and 2 percent when the child was four years old. Picture books were bought at the rate of one to two titles a month. They were selected by mothers, by children, by both parents and children, and by fathers, in that order. They were selected most often through browsing at book stores, followed by purchases based on book reviews in newspapers and magazines. Other sources were rarely used. The majority of mothers (74 percent) thought that picture books were expensive, and only 12 percent answered that they were reasonable. Fifty-nine percent of the mothers wanted less expensive picture books, even though the appearance might not be as good. On the other hand, 31 percent wanted sturdy, long-lasting books even though they might be a little more expensive.

Sawada and others (3) reported an analysis of the elements of picture books which interest children. The study was made through 1) a content analysis of eight picture books, and 2) recording responses of 60 preschool children during and after the telling of the stories in the picture books. Positive reactions such as "expressions of surprise" or "comments about the plot" occurred during the storytelling when there were 1) unexpected happenings in the story (unrealistic or imaginary contents), 2) settings similar to those in the children's experiences, 3) repetition of phrases, and 4) awe-inspiring scenes. Negative reactions during the telling of the story, such as "not looking at the books" or "not concentrating," were observed when the elements just mentioned were not present. Immediately following the storytelling session, the children showed superior recall of, and asked more questions about, stories whose contents elicited positive reactions during the telling. When the children ranked the books one week later, it was these same stories in almost every case which qualified as "most interesting."

In the study by Takagi and others (6), an experimental group of 11 three year old children was told a Japanese story, "Sorairo no tane," which was new to them, a total of three times with a three- or four-day interval between each telling.

The verbal and behavioral responses of the children during the recitation of the story were observed and classified. Tests of their memory of the story were given individually three months after the third telling. A control group of 9 three year olds was told the same story once, and their recall was tested three months later. During the first storytelling to the experimental group, negative reactions such as "not concentrating" and "extraneous talking during the story" were observed very frequently, while such positive reactions as "verbal responses to the contents of the story" were rare. During the second storytelling session, the children showed more positive and fewer negative reactions than during the first session. There were no differences between the frequencies of positive and negative reactions for the second and third sessions. Positive verbal responses were most frequently observed in the second session, while they were rare in the first session. The experimental group obtained higher scores on the memory test than did the control group.

The Consumer Goods Research Institute conducted research on the so-called "first book." According to a report in the Yomiuri Newspaper (8), four monthly magazines and 1030 different titles of such books for children under three were available in Japan. They sold very well and the report said that 43 percent of babies under three months old had at least one book. Also, 43 percent of three to six months old, 72 percent of six to twelve months old, 90 percent of twelve to eighteen months old, and 95 percent of eighteen to twenty-four months old had one or more of these first books. The Institute reported that the following examples are representative of the children's reactions, by group, to this type of book:

>(*Five months old*) They looked at pictures with bright colors, smiled at the picture of a child and a face, and made attempts to hold the book although it was impossible.
>(*Seven months old*) They tried to turn the pages.
>(*Eight months old*) They were clearly pleased to be read to.
>(*Ten months old*) They repeated the spoken words uttered by parents. For example, when a picture of food

was shown to a child with the spoken word "uma uma," a baby word for food in Japanese, the child repeated that word and touched the spoon and the plate in the picture. *(Eleven months old)* They licked and bit pictures of cats' and rabbits' faces. They were fond of a picture of a car in which a family with two children were riding. Their preference often centered on a book of automobiles.

(Fourteen months old) These young children often selected a book of automobiles and asked their mother to speak about it.

(Nineteen months old) At this age, the children acted out the action of a picture of a scene from daily life. For example, children would pretend to telephone when they looked at a picture of someone telephoning.

(Twenty-four months old) The two year old children liked to read or look at a book alone, and when they found something familiar, they went to their mother to report the discovery.

(Twenty-six months old) At this age, the child could memorize the text of the book. When the mother attempted to begin to read the text to the child, the child could give the text before the mother could read it.

The Institute concluded that these first books should be given to children and be accompanied by appropriate reading and speaking by the parents.

Final Comments

There is no big or critical problem in beginning reading in Japan because of:

1. The use of Hiragana which is easy to learn.
2. Parents' (usually mothers') concerns about their children's reading.
3. The quantity and quality of publications for preschool children.

In Japan, the mothers' role in children's beginning reading is considered more important than any other factor. Mothers sometimes are too interested in their children's letter learning and force them to learn Hiragana. They have a deep concern about their children's beginning reading, but they do not know the proper ways to promote it. A mother who can select suitable books for her children, who reads and rereads these books to them, who speaks to them about these books, who does not force them to learn letters, who answers their questions with a smile, and who, herself, likes to read is the ideal profile of a mother whose children can easily start to learn reading naturally.

References

1. IZUMOJI, TAKESHI, MACHIKO TAKENOYA, and KAZUKO MITSUIS. "Mothers' Concern about Picture Books," Science of Reading, 19 (1975), 1-12. (In Japanese)
2. SAKAMOTO, TAKAHIKO. "The Psychology of Japanese Learning," Jido Shinri, 1972, 1315-1380. (In Japanese)
3. SAWADA, MIZUYA, and others. "An Analysis of Children's Interests in Picture Books," Science of Reading, 17 (1974), 81-93. (In Japanese)
4. SHUPPAN NENKAN HENSHU BU. "Shuppan Nenkan," Shuppan News Sha, 1976. (In Japanese)
5. SUGIYAMA, YOSHIYA, and TAKAKO SAITO. "Variables of Parent Reading in Relation to the Social Traits of Kindergarten Pupils," Science of Reading, 16 (1973), 121-130. (In Japanese)
6. TAKAGI, KAZUKO, and others. "Responses of Three Year Old Children to Storytelling of a Japanese Picture Book," Science of Reading, 18 (1975), 105-113. (In Japanese)
7. THE NATIONAL LANGUAGE RESEARCH INSTITUTE OF JAPAN. "Reading and Writing Ability in Preschool Children," Tokyo Shoseki, 1972. (In Japanese)
8. YOMIURI NEWSPAPER. "Books for Babies," Yomiuri Shimbun, April 18, 1977. (In Japanese)

Beginning Reading in North America

Lloyd O. Ollila
University of Victoria
Victoria, British Columbia
Canada

Joanne R. Nurss
Georgia State University
Atlanta, Georgia
United States of America

A Historical Perspective Starting at the Turn of the Century

Beginning Reading from 1880 to 1910

During this period, teachers initiated reading instruction when the child began grade one, generally at age six. Although some school districts had kindergartens, kindergarten attendance was not compulsory. (Indeed, kindergarten attendance in some parts of Canada and the United States has been made compulsory only in the past twenty years.) Therefore, children typically began school in grade one, and it became customary to begin reading instruction in grade one at the established age of six.

Although this custom of beginning reading at age six became firmly entrenched, it was not accepted by everyone. Huey (*33*) cited and agreed with Dewey (*13*) and Patrick (*45*) that physical, emotional, and intellectual maturity necessary for successful reading would not be reached by the majority of children until eight years of age. Instead of beginning reading at age six, the child should be "acquiring [his] own experiences and developing wants that will in time make reading a natural and meaningful process" (*33*:303). Dewey (*13*) had written earlier:

> While there are exceptions, present physiological knowledge points to the age of about eight years as early enough for anything more than an incidental attention to visual and written language forms....

Dewey goes beyond this to suggest that some bright, mature children will naturally begin reading at home well before age six. The important ingredients for beginning reading are interest and motivation nurtured in a naturalistic setting— preferably the home. The school was struggling with tasks that could be handled more "naturally and effectively" by the home. The child "must have a 'personal hunger' for what is read"—something which would occur from seeing books used and enjoyed. Delaying instruction until age eight would allow time for this "personal hunger" to emerge in most children, thereby dramatically increasing success and the enjoyment of school reading. At this age, children would surpass mechanical, rote reading and understand and think about written content.

Although beginning reading instruction for all six year old children was questioned, little was done to change this in the schools. Few research findings had been gathered and there was an apparent lapse of interest in the subject.

How did children begin to read at the turn of the century? At this time educators across Europe and North America were influenced by a man named Johann Herbert, who felt that the teaching of literature should be emphasized in the schools. Reading materials became vehicles for teaching children this literature. Smith (*52*) describes the popular procedure of introducing grade one children to reading. The teacher would have a basic reader filled with folktales such as "The Little Red Hen." The children would first memorize the story, and then dramatize it. Finally, they would practice until they mastered reading the story. The whole class was involved in this "reading" period once each day. There would be another period devoted to memorizing phonetic families such as *at, cat, bat.* Gradually, children learned how to read.

Beginning Reading from 1910 to 1925

The fifteen year period between 1910 and 1925 saw the roots of a number of innovations that would influence beginning reading for much of this century. In 1910, Thorndike developed some scales of handwriting, marking the beginning of the scientific movement in education. Tests and other measures were used to obtain a variety of information about how children were doing in schools and how effectively different subjects were being taught. This scientific movement influenced reading research. Smith (52) reports that prior to 1910 there were only 34 studies done in reading, but by 1924 there were 436 studies. A number of school systems conducted achievement surveys at the end of grade one. Often these surveys showed that many children were failing grade one because they had not learned how to read. Educators such as Dickson (15) and Holmes (32) attributed this failure in reading to the fact that the children were not ready to learn to read when the teacher first began reading instruction.

This popular belief in reading readiness was based on the psychological publications of Gesell (26) and the Gesell Institute. During this time, Gesell's research focused on describing maturation in terms of developmental stages. This concept of development was supported by the research of McGraw (40), who concluded that practice would not hasten the developmental process. The development of motor skills seemed to explain the development of intellectual skills, so McGraw felt that time was the cure to a child's lack of reading readiness.

Reading instruction was delayed for children assessed as not ready. Many educators felt that this postponement and reliance on time and maturation would ensure more children of a successful beginning reading experience.

Although this was the popular view, there was a certain minority who believed that reading readiness had its foundation in the child's earlier learning experiences. The specific term "readiness" appeared in American education in 1925 in the widely read Yearbook of the National Society for the Study of Education. In fact, there was an entire chapter containing suggestions on developing reading readiness. Though North

American educators use many of these suggestions in their readiness training today, at the time of their publication the ideas were mostly ignored as they did not conform to popular concepts.

By 1925, the teaching of literature method was supplanted by other methods—most notably the silent reading approach. Although a few educators took an extreme view with no oral reading during the reading period, most teachers of beginning reading used the silent reading method to supplement their oral reading lessons. One way of teaching silent reading began with the presentation of a simple sentence needing an action response. For instance, the teacher would write "Jump up and down" on the blackboard. The teacher would then hint that the words were "something somebody in the class could do." The children would try to guess but if no one came up with the answer, the teacher would whisper it to a child who would demonstrate the action. Then the other children would discover what the sentence said. Seatwork used with this method might consist of short sentences in which the child would have to follow simple directions, such as: "Draw a duck and color it yellow."

Phonetic instruction began during the first three or four weeks of grade one. The children were first introduced to the sounds of letters and combinations by the teacher emphasizing the same sounds in rhymes and jingles.

Experience charts or stories written jointly by teachers and children began to be used by teachers during this period; however, most teachers still commenced reading with textbook materials. Classroom developed materials did not become popular until later.

Beginning Reading from 1925 to 1940

The scientific movement in education continued to influence beginning reading. Many reading researchers showed interest in isolating the main readiness factors. Out of this interest in isolating key factors came several studies which proposed that a certain mental age was necessary for success in learning to read. Dickson (15) reported that children who failed grade one had a mental age of less than six years. It was suggested that a basic requirement for beginning reading should be a specific mental age. Reading instruction should be postponed until this mental age was reached. This view of readiness remained popular and influential among practitioners and researchers for some time. The view was crystallized in the well publicized study by Morphett and Washburne (44:55). These two researchers compared the reading achievement and mental abilities of all grade one children in the Winnetka, Illinois, schools. They reported:

> ... the children who had a mental age of six years and six months made far better progress than did the less mature children and practically as satisfactory progress as did the children of a higher mental age.

The researchers concluded that successful reading would be more likely to occur when its instruction was postponed until children reached a mental age of six years and six months.

Although their conclusions may have held true in Winnetka, given the materials in use and the methods employed, their view that children should wait to learn to read until they attain a mental age of 6.5 is a fallacy that appears to have been readily accepted by many educators.

Contrary to this popular view, Gates (24) hypothesized that mental age was arbitrarily linked to reading achievement. He believed that the necessary mental age for successful reading was influenced by such factors as materials, teaching strategies, teacher effectiveness, class size, and preparatory work. To assess the various factors, he worked with groups of students under four different conditions. The first group was supplied with regular textbooks, but also with supplementary practice and teach-and-test materials specifically designed for the study. After their training, the students' reading grades were correlated with their mental ages with r = .62. The second group was taught by teachers judged to be more expert than average and supplied with a "considerable body of experimental materials" developed by Gates and his colleagues. The correlation between reading grade and mental age was r = .55. The third group received better than average teachers and textbook materials, but did not have many supplementary materials. The correlation between reading grade and mental age was r = .44. The fourth group consisted of two large classes taught by teachers judged to be inferior and operating with less than adequate materials and facilities. The instruction was primarily "whole group" with little individualized instruction and produced the lowest correlation between mental age and reading grade, with r = .34. Gates found that the correlation between the two factors was highest in classes with the best instruction (*24*:62):

> The magnitude of the correlation seems to vary directly with the effectiveness of the provision for individual differences in the classroom....
> It is impossible to set up, once and for all a stipulated list of particular requirements for successful work in beginning reading in general.

Teachers must assess specific materials or programs to determine what mental age, background experience, and aptitudes are required for their successful mastery. It is possible to organize materials to ensure reading mastery for children with a mental age of 5.0. Gates did not believe this was necessarily desirable. The optimum mental age for beginning reading needed to be examined by thorough studies of the developmental stages. It is unfortunate that this enlightening study was largely ignored, as it contradicted the then popular trend.

Since popular belief held that a mental age of 6.5 was necessary for the child to achieve success in beginning reading, researchers had to devise reliable measures to determine when a child had reached this age. Consequently, readiness testing became an essential part of beginning reading and has continued in popularity in North America to the present day. Readiness tests were used as early as 1927 and since then they have varied considerably in their content and emphasis. Typical subskill measures included rate of learning, phoneme correspondence, rhyming, visual motor coordination, listening comprehension, letter recognition, numerical concepts, visual matching of forms, and vocabulary knowledge. Subskill scores were added together so teachers could get a global score which tended to divide children into one of two categories: "ready to begin reading" or "not ready."

Readiness tests were given at the start of grade one. For the many children who were not ready according to these tests, reading readiness programs were developed. With few guidelines to follow, many varied tests were developed and implemented, depending on educator preferences and interests.

One of the early books on reading readiness was published by Harrison in 1936 (*30*). She describes types of instruction that would foster reading readiness. She points out that preparatory instruction must be done prior to beginning reading and that it could "form a portion" of the kindergarten curriculum if school entrance began there. Otherwise, it should be carried out in grade one. Harrison (*30*:32) quoted Paul McKee's list of seven major fields of instruction including the following:

1. Providing pupils with real, varied, and rich experiences essential to the getting of meaning from materials to be read.
2. Training in the ability to do problematic thinking.
3. Training in the speaking of simple English sentences.
4. The development of a wide speaking vocabulary.
5. Training in accurate enunciation and pronunciation.
6. The development of a desire to read.
7. Training in the organization and recognition of sequential ideas.

During this time period also, commercial reading textbook publishers (Scott, Foresman and Row Peterson) began to produce accompanying "readiness books" which Harrison (*31*:49) describes as presenting:

The necessary conceptual content for early reading in the series by means of pictures and suggested topics for discussion, as well as other types of materials which may be used in connection with the other instructional jobs of the readiness period.

Beginning reading instruction used a wide variety of approaches. Smith (*52*:232) analyzed eight teacher manuals of this period and found the following procedures:

1. Reading charts and compositions composed by the children about their experiences.
2. Reading Mother Goose rhymes, plus stories the children composed.
3. Reading and performing action sentences, plus reading stories the children composed.
4. Reading and performing action sentences, plus reading rhymes (not Mother Goose).
5. Dramatizing the pictures, phrases, and sentences concerning them.
6. Telling the first book story, then dramatizing and reproducing it.

7. Reading from prepared charts containing the early primer vocabulary.

Experience charts were gaining acceptance at this time. Commercial publishers began to market preprimers designed to be a half step between prereading activities and reading primers. Many reading authorities agreed with Gates (23) in his *First Grade Manual* that the teaching of phonics by extensive drills should be initiated later in grade one than had been the case. Reading authorities also began giving greater attention to grouping beginning readers into ability groups to adapt to individual differences.

Beginning Reading from 1940 to 1960

The technological revolution gained momentum with the birth of the atomic age early in the 1940s. This tremendous influence, along with the second world war, made for unique circumstances in the 1940s and 1950s. The concept of readiness had already reached its zenith but continued to dominate research and practice in beginning reading.

The war effort made teachers hard to find and research and instructional materials even scarcer. The thrust in reading research was more for the adult population who needed to be informed of victories, losses, and defense measures—little energy was spent on the beginning reader. However, some important works were published. Notable professional books included *Teaching the Child to Read (8), Teaching Primary Reading (16),* and *Improvement of Basic Reading Abilities (19).*

The reading program was divided into reading instruction and literature at this time. More teacher manuals became available, accompanying two kinds of readiness materials designed for individual and group work. The content of readers tended to be realistic and vividly illustrated with the vocabulary greatly reduced. Smith (50) reported that there were approximately 289 words introduced into beginning readers in 1931, while in 1940 the number dropped to 122. This meant that word mastery involved meaning and use of the same words in several different contexts. Rote learning of vocabulary was on the decline. Reading was meshing with the language arts and general communication skills of listening and speaking.

Teachers and researchers were beginning to recognize that readiness belonged at all levels—not just at the start of schooling. This more global view encouraged diverse methods of instruction. Individual differences, including differing rates of maturity, were gaining recognition. Reading disabilities were no longer attributed to lack of readiness alone—psychiatric insights led to psychological treatments (41, 47). Other factors involved in readiness were recognized.

It is significant that interest in these other factors was initiated in the early 1940s and incubated after the war. Sullivan and McCarthy (54) considered important factors influencing readiness and identified the home conditions, meaning vocabulary or experiences, physiological maturity, ability to see similarities and differences, object discrimination, and motor coordination. Cultural influences were investigated by Dennis and Dennis (12). Gates (25) recommended the use of several readiness tests to reach a reliable score for individuals. He concluded that readiness testing should involve diagnosis and appraisal, tests of general intelligence, sensory equipment, speech, and a health examination, along with the familiar battery of readiness tests. He suggested these varied tests would indicate immediate needs that should be met before going on to "typical" readiness procedures which included adjusting to school situations; learning to use classroom equipment; building a background of common information; developing knowledge of specific and useful facts; developing word sounds, oral usages, and an interest in reading. Gates believed this to be a smoother, more meaningful, progression which was less likely to confuse or frighten children at the outset of their reading and general school instruction. He implied that readiness involved many aspects of the individual.

Evans (21) looked at kindergarten procedures to consider their potential in developing readiness by "enlarging the child's experiences and quickening his observation." This concern was supported by Kottmeyer (38:355) who believed "the city systems have increasingly large numbers of children entering first grade, who are, as a group, less ready to learn to read than formerly." Readiness was not simply related to mental age. Experience through time was proving its complex nature. Brownell (9:445-446) summarized these revelations:

Readiness, in a word, is seen to be far from sacrosanct in its development; it is rather, amenable to stimulation, direction, and control to an extent far greater than is assumed by those who rely upon anatomical maturation.

The 1950s studied cultural factors more closely, systematically seeking ways to equalize differences. Young and Gaier (*59*) identified social class differences and general home stability as being important for readiness. Almy (*2*) along with Sheldon and Carillo (*49*) demonstrated that cultural factors, such as family size, number of books in the home, and parents' education, correlated with reading success.

Durrell (*20*) concluded that one quarter of the children doing poorly were intellectually capable but were lacking in specific background experiences necessary for reading. These experiences needed to be provided by the schools. In 1955, Flesch published his influential book, *Why Johnny Can't Read*, in which he encouraged parents to start phonics instruction in the home *prior* to grade one—contrary to the mental age advocates. This book reflected a trend that supported not only the cultural investigations of the early 1950s, but also the relatively new and successful reading instruction carried out with children aged two to five years. Burke (*10*) demonstrated that three and four year olds could learn to read, spell, and write using Montessori materials. Moore (*42*) worked successfully with young children and computerized typewriters. Kohlberg (*37*) suggested that reading and writing were low level sensory motor skills requiring practice that bored children aged six to eight but challenged very young children. Readiness was going beyond maturation, mental age, and items on readiness tests. Significantly, although published after Sputnik (1957), this research was being carried out at the time of the launching—an event which helped these "new" ideas to gain recognition. They could not be ignored as they had been in the past. New directions were needed.

Ausubel (*6:246*) defined readiness as "the adequacy of existing capacity in relation to the demands of a given learning task." The question no longer was "Is the child ready?" but "Is the child ready for this particular kind and quality of instruction?" Education was ready to take a closer, more carefully focused look at aspects of readiness.

The late 1950s saw a change in attitude toward education. Gates (*24*) and Huey (*33*) were being reconsidered and used for further research. Environment was gaining more importance than heredity; growth and development were discussed in terms of environment, learning, and practice; children's intellectual development was of major concern; and children's early (prefirst grade) years were thought to be of special importance to intellectual functioning. This new and wider approach is clearly demonstrated in the definition of readiness provided in the *Encyclopedia of Educational Research* (7:1081-1082).

> To be completely ready for an educational activity or learning experience a child must want to learn, be sufficiently mature physiologically, possess appropriate mental abilities, and finally have had the right kind of educational experiences.

Reading readiness was no longer a small area dependent solely on a specific mental age. Researchers generally admitted its complex nature and the need for serious investigations of all relevant factors. Huey and Gates were no longer ignored. Sputnik forced educators to consider all possibilities to maximize educational efficiency.

Beginning Reading from 1960 to 1980

Beginning reading instruction in the United States and Canada in 1980 reflects the educational research and technological developments of the post-Sputnik period. The age at which reading is introduced, the role of parents in teaching reading, the instructional materials, methods, organization, and evaluation all have changed over the past twenty years.

Age

Children in North America enter primary school at six years of age. Most school systems offer a half-day kindergarten program for five year olds. Entrance into school is once a year in September and, in most school systems, the child must be six years old by the following December in order to begin first grade. The lay assumption, and the one held by most six year olds, is that children will be taught to read in first grade. Although this is the case for most children, some children can read when they enter first grade and others do not learn until later. The concept of continuous progress has been generally adopted; children who are not successful in mastering beginning reading skills in first grade move on to second grade where instruction in beginning reading continues from the point reached in first grade (*34*).

The understanding that children can learn to read before beginning first grade stems largely from Durkin's well-known investigation of early readers (*17*). In two studies carried out in California and in New York in the 1960s, Durkin surveyed incoming first graders during the first few weeks of school. In her second study, she found that about 4 percent could already read, obtaining reading grade level scores from 1.4 to 5.2. She followed these children for several years and discovered that the early readers continued to read as well as or better than a matched comparison group of nonearly readers. In no way did the children appear to be harmed by their early reading adventures. In fact, many of them were helped by this "head start." Durkin's study freed parents and educators to consider helping children with reading before they entered first grade.

In the early 1970s, King and Friesen (*35*) reported a study of Canadian children who could read when they entered kindergarten at age five years. They found that approximately 0.75 percent could read at the first grade level or above. Although this is not a large percentage, it is interesting to note that these early readers had many characteristics in common with the six year old children in Durkin's study. For example, they preferred quiet games and handwork, were taken to a library more often, and watched television less than a randomly selected control group of nonreaders. The early readers made large gains in oral reading in a year of instruction during kindergarten.

Durkin's study came at a time when there was renewed interest in kindergarten and prekindergarten education in North America. Montessori classes became popular; readiness or reading workbooks were introduced into many kindergartens; and phonics programs were added. By the midseventies, most kindergartens had phonics programs which taught children to discriminate and name letters, discriminate sounds, and match sounds and letters. Unfortunately, in some school systems the first grade program and materials were simply moved down to the kindergarten. In other systems, however, an integrated language arts program was developed resembling the one described by Durkin (*18*). Her program was based upon a traditional kindergarten program of play with trucks, blocks, dolls, dress-up clothes, and housekeeping toys; physical actitivies on climbing and riding toys; and art, music, and stories. These activities were supplemented by an integrated language arts program of conversation and sharing groups, listening activities, a writing center in which the children learned to name and write letters and numerals, and reading activities in which they learned sight words related to current interests and read homemade books and other reading materials. It is this latter model of kindergarten prereading and reading activities which is advocated by many American reading professors and which is implemented in some schools in North America.

Another factor in lowering the age at which North American children begin to read has been the new concept of readiness discussed earlier. MacGinitie (*39*:399) highlights the readiness/beginning reading continuum by saying "... when a child is taught a little, he is then ready for a little more." No longer is the kindergarten year seen as a readiness period to be followed by an introduction to reading in the first months of first grade. Rather kindergarten and first grade are seen as a continuum along which children move, developing prereading and beginning reading skills according to their own time-tables. Although some schools still have a fixed readiness period in kindergarten or first grade, many have adopted the more flexible notion of a continuum of skills development throughout the kindergarten and first grade years.

Role of Parents

One of the most dramatic changes in beginning reading in North America in the 1960s was in the role of parents. Instead of fostering a "hands off" policy which had been advocated widely (*53*), parents are now invited to participate in teaching their children to read. They are urged to talk with and listen to their children in order to help them develop oral language skills, to read to their children regularly, and to answer their questions about words and letters. Frequently, these activities encourage children to begin to recognize words, read advertisements and labels, and write their own names (46, 57). There are many commercial materials available for parents to purchase to help their children. Supermarkets sell prereading activity books and paperback story books. Toy stores offer a wide variety of educational toys and games to develop fine motor skills, visual discrimination, vocabulary, and concepts. There are also books and materials specifically designed for parents to use in teaching their children to read. These are not advocated by most reading personnel because, in their enthusiasm to help their children, parents frequently push them beyond their interest and developmental levels, thus causing frustration and failure.

Many schools now have parent involvement programs during which parents are encouraged to visit the school, participate in special activities, or become volunteer aides in the classroom. Volunteers are usually trained by the school or system personnel to read stories, transcribe stories children dictate to them, supervise independent activities, engage children in special projects, make materials planned by the classroom teacher, or work with small groups of children who need extra practice in certain reading skills. Parents usually do not work in their own child's class. These parents provide a valuable service to the classroom teacher, particularly to those who do not have the assistance of an aide. In addition, parents gain an understanding of the school's reading program and become good ambassadors to the community and to other parents (58).

Some of the federally funded programs for low socio-economic areas, such as Head Start and Follow Through, have parent involvement programs in which home visitors take instructional kits into each home once a week. The parents teach these concepts and skills, many of which are related to beginning reading, to their own children and discuss the results with the home visitor each week. These visitors may also take library books and/or toys into the homes. In these programs, the children are helped to learn essential skills and concepts and the parents learn additional parenting skills which can be used with other children in the family.

In the United States, education is largely controlled by the local community of which the beginning readers' parents are members. Funding is primarily from local, city, or township taxes, augmented by state and federal funds. Most federal funds are allocated through the individual states, however, so there is relatively little national control of educational policy, curriculum, or materials. In Canada there is both local and provincial control of educational funding and policy but, similarly, no federal control. In the United States and parts of Canada, the local school system is run by an elected board of education which "hires and fires" the superintendent of schools. This arrangement allows for direct public influence on the policies of the local schools. If the parents and community do not like a program (for instance, the beginning reading program), they can contact their elected board members and make known their desires for a change. If they are not satisfied by the results of such persuasion, at the next election they can choose board members with policies more to their liking. This system means that educators must be accountable for their instructional efforts and must be constantly responsive to community standards.

Currently, a number of Canadian and American school systems are engaged in curriculum reform known as "back to basics." This usually means a beginning reading program that is heavily phonetic and uses reading materials with stories which teach patriotism and moral development. In addition, penmanship, arithmetic, and discipline are emphasized. This back to basics movement is community/parent instigated rather than being the result of educational research or theory (43). In other words, American parents do have a role in deciding how their children are to be taught to read as well as in helping them to begin reading.

Instructional Methods and Materials

Beginning reading instruction in North America is skills oriented. The most commonly used material for teaching reading is the basal reader. Prior to the 1970s, basal readers consisted of readiness workbooks, preprimers, primers, and first readers for the first grade. These books were accompanied by workbooks, large pictures, and flash cards for practicing word recognition. Generally, they introduced a carefully controlled vocabulary based upon the oral vocabulary of five year olds. Many words were phonetically irregular and were taught by look-say methods with frequent and systematic repetitions. Word analysis skills were introduced very slowly. Basal series have been justifiably criticized as being racist, sexist, and showing only middle class, small town, and rural families. The stories also have been criticized as uninteresting, written in unnatural language, and too dependent upon illustrations. Basal readers were often used in a lockstep fashion with the teacher's main pressure being to get every child to read "on grade level," meaning to read the appropriate grade level book. It was equally as bad to have a child "above grade level" as it was to have one "below grade level." Reading lessons as outlined in the teacher's manual consisted of introducing new words, motivating the children to read the story, guiding silent reading (page by page), posing comprehension questions following each page, reading orally "round robin" with the children taking turns reading one page around the reading circle, practicing on a relevant reading skill, and completing workbook pages and/or board work exercises to practice the new words and the reading skill. Fortunately, much of this has now changed.

Most basal readers still provide a comprehensive, sequential system for reading instruction, but the books now have stories which show a variety of races; women and girls in an equally favorable light to men and boys; a variety of socioeconomic classes; different urban settings, as well as towns and rural areas; and a variety of family patterns. Vocabulary control has been relaxed, stories are more interesting, language is more natural, and phonics instruction has been added earlier and in greater quantity. Most systems use levels instead of grades to try to overcome the lockstep labeling of children. A wide variety of additional materials such as cassettes, storybooks, filmstrips, puzzles, games, worksheets, and pictures are available to accompany most basal series.

The success of any reading program is dependent upon the teacher. In the past, many teachers misused the traditional basal series by adhering to the manual in a rigid manner. Teachers using the less structured newer materials often fail to provide an orderly sequential development of word analysis and vocabulary skills. The levels can be misused just as the grade designations were. No matter how carefully beginning reading materials are designed, the teacher is the key factor in children's learning.

Another change in current basal reading materials is the diversity in methodologies now available. In addition to analytic phonics methods, there are series using synthetic phonics methods, linguistic methods, programed methods, and a modified alphabet. Individualized reading and language experience approaches are also used in North American schools.

The analytic or meaning-emphasis approach to beginning reading stresses comprehension of the initial reading material, while the synthetic or code-emphasis approach stresses decoding of the initial material. Austin (5:506) says that "... few educators will disagree that reading is meaningful interpretation of written and printed symbols." The differences lie in the timing and in the emphasis on comprehension. The analytic phonics or meaning-emphasis method introduces children to some words by sight, emphasizing the meaning of the words, phrases, and sentences in the books. When the children know several words which begin with the same consonant (top, toy, to, take), they are encouraged to note the similarities of beginning letters and beginning sounds and to conclude that the sound /t/ is usually represented by the letter "t." The synthetic phonics or decoding method, on the other hand, introduces the unstressed vowel sounds and a few consonant sounds in isolation, teaching the children to discriminate the sound and to associate it with the appropriate letter. Beginning reading material consists largely of words formed by blending these sounds (for example, /a/, /m/, /t/, /r/—mat, rat, tam, ram, at, am). There have been many attempts to compare the effectiveness of these methods with a variety of conclusions. One frequently cited comparison (11) reviewed research on the code- and meaning-emphasis approaches and found that 1) the code-emphasis approaches produced better overall reading achievement by the beginning of fourth grade (nine year olds) than did the meaning-emphasis approaches and 2) code-emphasis approaches were better for children with below average and average intelligence and from low socioeconomic levels, but meaning-emphasis approaches were better for children of high intelligence and from middle and high socioeconomic levels. The debate is by no means concluded.

The linguistic approaches grew out of the work of linguists who noted that both the analytic and synthetic phonic approaches distort the phonological sounds. One type of linguistic series introduces word families in which substitutions can be made without distorting the sounds. For example, "The frog on a log with a dog." Some linguistic series use nonsense words which illustrate the decoding principle being taught but convey no meaning. The idea is to teach decoding first and to introduce comprehension later. There are many variations of the linguistic approach currently in use (4).

Programed approaches to beginning reading break down the process into small steps. Each step is presented as an item which is read (stimulus) and for which a response must be selected. The program provides immediate feedback (indicating whether the response is correct or incorrect). Reinforcement is given and additional practice may be indicated if the children make errors. Programed reading materials are usually in workbook format, but may be in a machine or computer. Students proceed at their own pace, but all children complete essentially the same material; thus the pace is individualized, but the activities are not. Programed materials are popular in behaviorally oriented classrooms.

In the late 1960s the Initial Teaching Alphabet materials (i.t.a.) from England were modified and an American i.t.a. basal series appeared. The alphabet was modified to a one-to-one phoneme-grapheme correspondence, thus reducing the task of learning to decode. The readers use a meaning-emphasis basal reader format. After children have mastered reading with i.t.a., they are given transition material to learn how to decode traditional orthography. Although i.t.a. is still used in a few systems, it has never been widely used in North America and seems to be decreasing in popularity.

Two other approaches used in North America are the individualized reading approach and the language experience approach. Individualized reading makes use of a wide variety of trade books from which children select their own reading books. The teacher listens to the children read, asks comprehension questions, and assists with appropriate skills. This method is widely used as a supplementary method in connection with a basal or language experience approach. When used alone, it places a great responsibility upon the teacher to be aware of the reading skills and their sequence, to be able to diagnose "on the spot," and to prescribe appropriate skill activities individually. Most school systems find that these demands are too severe for the average or inexperienced teacher, making this method less effective when used as the only reading approach. However, the emphasis on meaning, the interest sustained by the child's selection of the reading books, and the personal meeting with the teacher all commend this approach as one part of a reading program. The advent of a multitude of children's literature titles in inexpensive paperback format and of an interesting variety of "easy-to-read" books has made individualized reading even more popular with beginning reading teachers (29).

The language experience approach to reading is one in which children produce their own reading materials: dictating simple stories (initially a few words or a phrase) to the teacher, seeing them written down, and then reading them to the teacher. Ultimately, children write their own stories, produce books, and read them to other children. The teacher must develop a sequence of skills from each child's work and must assist the child in going from reading sentences and phrases to recognizing individual words. The language experience approach makes good use of children's oral language, integrates writing with reading, grows out of the children's own experiences, and is therefore meaningful. Language experience is used as the only approach to teaching reading in a few instances in North America. More typically, however, it is used in connection with individualized reading and a sequential skills program.

There is sufficient diversity in the United States and Canada for it to be a bit presumptuous to speak of the "typical" beginning reading program. However, in many schools children are introduced to beginning reading by learning to recognize some common words at sight (for example, their names, words related to a unit of study, words for colors or shapes, and words appearing around the room on a calendar, helper chart, etc.). Simultaneously, children learn letter sounds, letter names, and sound-letter correspondences. From that beginning, children are introduced to a basal series and taught the vocabulary and sequential skills of that series. As children develop some reading proficiency, they are encouraged to engage in an individualized reading program. Thoughout the beginning reading period, children will have been encouraged to write sentences and stories to read and perhaps develop into books. The basal reader phonics program will be taught and applied in reading library books, writing stories, and playing word games.

In recent years, the systems concept has become prevalent in education and in beginning reading. A number of basal series have been developed along this line, as have many curriculum guides and special programs. In a systems approach the broad objectives are stated, the task to be accomplished is analyzed, the individual is assessed to determine which component parts (skills) have been mastered, the specific instructional objectives are stated, the instructional activities are presented, and an evaluation measure is given to determine whether the objectives have been reached. If so, the learners are taken to the next step; if not, they are "recycled" for further instruction and/or practice. The well-developed system has the goals for learning to read analyzed into the component parts in such a way that, upon completion of the system, children are proficient readers. Most schools and teachers use some modification of this systems approach (such as a diagnostic-prescriptive approach) to teaching beginning reading. The teacher has the whole process in mind and the children are made aware of the meaningful nature of the reading process; however, at any point in time, the activities might be based on one small step within the process.

The decision as to which of these methods or materials will be used for beginning reading is usually made by the local school system. The school principal may make modifications to adapt the reading program to the local community. Individual classroom teachers are given a basic curriculum to follow and a set textbook to use, however, with relatively little room for individual choice. Both Canada and the United States have sizeable bilingual and/or non-English speaking communities (French in Quebec and Spanish in New York, Miami, and Los Angeles). In Canada, French speaking schools have been established and French speaking children are taught to read initially in French. Later many are taught to read in English, although dual French speaking and English speaking secondary schools and universities make it possible for a Canadian to obtain a monolingual education in either French or English (3). In the United States there are some Spanish speaking or bilingual (Spanish-English) schools in which children learn to read in Spanish. In most instances, however, Spanish speaking children are taught English as a second language and then given reading instruction in English. No Spanish speaking secondary schools or universities exist in the United States (except in Puerto Rico). Therefore, native Spanish speakers must learn English to complete their education.

Instructional Organization

Most North American elementary schools have single age classes taught by one teacher. The child moves to another class and another teacher each year. Classes are coeducational with mixed ability groups. Generally, classes are self-contained at the primary level with the classroom teacher teaching all subjects. The teacher's role is relatively central, especially in reading instruction. Direct instruction in reading is usually given to small groups of children. Typically, there will be three or four small groups for reading instruction in a first grade classroom. This intraclass grouping is done mainly by reading achievement level. Instruction in basic skills, practice in word recognition, and guided silent reading followed by comprehension questions will be given. Fortunately, round robin oral reading is beginning to disappear in favor of children taking turns in reading individually to the teacher or to other children. Children do oral reading for many different purposes; for example, reading directions for making something, finding a specific bit of information needed for a group project, locating a favorite passage in a story, or getting a message on a poster. While one group works with the teacher, the other groups engage in learning center activities, library reading, or written independent work. Too often, however, the same workbook pages or duplicated worksheets are provided for every child within a subgroup. A few first grade classrooms also have manipulative toys; housekeeping and block centers; and creative areas with paint, water, or sand.

In some schools, children are grouped by reading achievement levels into an interclass grouping scheme. All the children from the primary grades reading at the same level join for instruction in one teacher's room. Although this method has the advantage of reducing the range of reading levels with which one teacher must cope, there still are individual levels and learning rates present. This also means that reading must be taught in a rigid time frame which makes it difficult to coordinate instruction with the other language arts and subject areas. For these reasons, this type of organization is less common than intraclass grouping.

Open-plan arrangements, similar to those found in many British infant schools, have been developed in Canada and the United States in recent years. In some cases, buildings built in the open-plan format contain self-contained classrooms in spite of the architectural arrangements. In other cases, the physical space, staffing, and schedule have been modified to allow an informal, less structured organization. In a few cases, family grouping exists so that a class may contain children of several ages. Extensive research comparing this arrangement to more traditional organization has not yet been reported. However, a few studies have indicated that the open approach is beneficial to children's affective and creative development, but is not as successful in teaching them to read as is a more traditional organization (56).

Theoretical Background

The beginning reading methods common in the United States and Canada grow out of a theoretical understanding of reading which distinguishes between beginning reading and proficient reading. Although most American reading researchers would define reading as the process of understanding or comprehending a printed message, many see beginning reading as the process of mastering decoding skills and then applying them to "get meaning from the written message." Samuels (48) says that reading subskills (which are emphasized in beginning reading instruction) are simply a means to an end. The end, of course, is meaning. However, before the whole can be dealt with, the parts must be mastered.

The subskills important to beginning reading include visual discrimination, auditory discrimination and blending, and auditory-visual integration (all of which are essential for decoding words) and oral language development such as vocabulary, concepts, language structure, and reasoning (essential for comprehending the total written message—phrases, sentences, and paragraphs). Most American beginning reading practices are based upon this subskill analysis of the beginning reading process, teaching the two groups of subskills simultaneously.

In recent years, several American researchers (28, 50, 51) have suggested that even beginning reading is a process of extracting meaning from the written message. Goodman describes reading as a "psycholinguistic guessing game" in which the meaning of a passage is reconstructed by readers via the meaning in their minds (28). Smith (50:230) says that readers "predict their way through a passage." He also suggests that the teacher's primary instructional task is to "respond to what the child is trying to do" (51:195). Evidence that beginning readers can and perhaps do learn to read by seeing the meaningful whole instead of mastering the component parts comes from young children who are either self-taught or who learn by looking at books, writing stories, and "reading" along with competent readers (55). In discussing competence and performance in reading, Kinsbourne (36) notes that children can master all of the subskills (pass all the criterion measures) and still not be able to read, that is, not be able to integrate the subskills into the process. The North American professional literature (journals and conference papers) now is suggesting that beginning reading practices should use a meaningful, holistic approach rather than a subskills approach. School practice reflects this change in the increased use of meaningful context to teach subskills. At this time, however, most North American children are taught to read by skills-oriented approaches and materials. Adams, Anderson, and Durkin (1:20) suggest that beginning reading is not simply a letter and word discrimination process nor simply a psycholinguistic guessing game. Rather, they suggest that beginning reading is an interactive process in which discrimination and prediction occur simultaneously. They state that successful reading is dependent on meaning, both in the text and in the reader's mind.

It will be interesting to see the research evidence produced to support each of these theoretical models of beginning reading and the subsequent influence of that research on instructional practices and published materials in North America.

Evaluation of Beginning Reading

Beginning reading programs are frequently evaluated by measuring the progress of the children during first grade. Traditionally, standardized reading achievement tests have been given to pupils at the end of first or second grade in most North American school systems. These summative measures are still in use for measuring the progress of individual pupils as well as classes, schools, and systems. They are supplemented in many systems, however, by formative measures such as informal reading inventories, miscue analyses, skills monitoring tests, and criterion-referenced tests.

Informal reading inventories are samples of the child's skill in silent and oral reading of graded passages from the basal series to be used in instruction. Reading is followed by standard comprehension questions. These inventories help a teacher place a child in a reading series level appropriate for instruction.

Miscue analysis, based upon the work of Goodman (27), gives the teacher a sample of children's oral reading with attention to the ways in which they approach words they do not recognize. Miscues are separated into those which make semantic sense, those which make syntactic sense, those which make phonemic sense, and those which make no sense at all.

Skills-monitoring tests and criterion-referenced tests are measures of specific objectives or subskills thought to be important to the reading process. Children are assessed on each separate subskill and only when they have mastered that subskill (met the criterion) is instruction given on the next subskill in the hierarchy. Many of these subskill tests are designed to accompany basal reader series, giving the teacher standard preassessment and postassessment for each instructional level in the series. In a number of school systems in the United States, criterion-referenced tests have been developed and implemented as measures of the standards of instruction and achievement in reading. In some states, pupils must pass a criterion-referenced reading test to graduate from secondary school.

Both formative and summative evaluation measures are important components of beginning reading programs in North America although their exact form and use vary from system to system.

Summary of the 1960s and 1970s

Formal reading instruction in Canada and the United States generally begins in the first grade so that most children learn to read at six years of age. Typically they are taught in a self-centered, age-graded class. Reading instruction is most likely to be in a subgroup of the class using basal readers which include a phonics program. Subskills in decoding and comprehension are taught and practiced in group and independent activities. The subskills program often is supplemented by a language experience program in which the children write stories or by an individualized program in which they read library books and supplementary readers. The reading program is coordinated with the total language arts program although separate instructional activities are provided for speaking and listening, penmanship, spelling, and literature. Continuous teacher assessment of each child's progress is usually augmented by summative evaluation (probably standardized measures) at the end of first grade.

Local communities vary on aspects of the above description, further emphasizing the strong local control of public education—including beginning reading—throughout North America.

References

1. ADAMS, M.J., R.C. ANDERSON, and D. DURKIN. "Beginning Reading: Theory and Practice," *Language Arts,* 55 (1978), 19-25
2. ALMY, M.C. "Children's Experiences Prior to First Grade and Success in Beginning Reading," *Teachers College Record,* 51 (1950), 392-393.
3. ANDERSON, N. *Studies in Multilingualism.* Leiden: E.J. Brill, 1969.
4. AUKERMAN, R.C. *Approaches to Beginning Reading,* Second Edition. New York: John Wiley, 1971.
5. AUSTIN, M.C. "United States," in J. Downing (Ed.), *Comparative Reading: Cross-National Studies of Behavior and Process in Reading and Writing.* New York: Macmillan, 1973.
6. AUSUBEL, D.P. "Viewpoint from Related Disciplines: Human Growth and Development," *Teachers College Record,* 60 (1959), 245-254.
7. BLAIR, G.M., and R.S. JONES. "Readiness," *Encyclopedia of Educational Research,* Third Edition. New York: Macmillan, 1960, 1081-1085.
8. BOND, G., and E. BOND. *Teaching the Child to Read.* New York: Macmillan, 1943.
9. BROWNELL, W.A. "Readiness for Subject Matter Learning," *National Education Association Journal,* 40 (1951), 445-446.
10. BURKE, O. "Whitby School," *Jubilee,* 6 (February 1959), 211-215.
11. CHALL, J. *Learning to Read: The Great Debate.* New York: McGraw-Hill, 1967.
12. DENNIS, W., and M.G. DENNIS. "Does Culture Appreciably Affect Patterns of Infant Behavior?" *Journal of Social Psycology,* 12 (1940), 305-317.
13. DEWEY, J. *New York Teachers' Monographs.* November 1898.
14. DICKSON, V.E. "What First Grade Children Can Do in School as Related to What is Shown By Mental Tests," *Journal of Educational Research,* June 1920, 475-480.
15. DICKSON, V.E. *Mental Tests and the Classroom Teacher.* New York: World Book, 1923.
16. DOLCH, E.W. *Teaching Primary Reading.* Champaign, Illinois: Garrard, 1941.
17. DURKIN, D. *Children Who Read Early,* New York: Teachers College Press, 1966.
18. DURKIN, D. *Teaching Them to Read.* Boston: Allyn and Bacon, 1970.
19. DURRELL, D. *Improvement of Basic Reading Abilities.* New York: World Book, 1940
20. DURRELL, D.D. "Learning Difficulties among Children of Normal Intelligence," *Elementary School Journal,* 55 (1954), 201-208.
21. EVANS, C. "Reading Readiness for the Kindergarten," *Elementary English,* 22 (March 1945), 143-146.
22. FLESCH, R. *Why Johnny Can't Read and What You Can Do about It.* New York: Harper and Row, 1955.
23. GATES, A.I., and M. HUBER. *The Work-Play Books, First Grade Manual.* New York: Macmillan, 1930.

24. GATES, A.I. "The Necessary Mental Age for Beginning Reading,"*Elementary School Journal,* 37 (March 1937), 497-508.
25. GATES, A.I. "A Further Evaluation of Reading Readiness Tests," *Elementary English,* 40 (1940), 577-591.
26. GESELL, A. *Infancy and Human Growth.* New York: Macmillan, 1928.
27. GOODMAN, K.S. "A Linguistic Study of Cues and Miscues in Reading," *Elementary English,* 42 (1965), 639-643.
28. GOODMAN, K.S. "Behind the Eye: What Happens in Reading," *Reading: Process and Program.* Urbana, Illinois: National Council of Teachers of English, 1970, 3-5.
29. HARRIS, L.A., and C.B. SMITH. *Reading Instruction: Diagnostic Teaching in the Classroom,* Second Edition. New York: Holt, Rinehart and Winston, 1976.
30. HARRISON, L. *Reading Readiness.* Boston: Houghton Mifflin, 1936.
31. HARRISON, L. *Reading Readiness,* Second Edition. Boston: Houghton Mifflin, 1939.
32. HOLMES, M.C. "Investigation of Reading Readiness of First Grade Entrants," *Childhood Education,* 111 (January 1927), 215-221.
33. HUEY, E.B. *The Psychology and Pedagogy of Reading.* New York: Macmillan, 1980.
34. KATZ, J. *Education in Canada.* Hamden, Connecticut: Archon Books, 1974.
35. KING, E.M., and D.T. FRIESEN. "Children Who Read in Kindergarten," *Alberta Journal of Educational Research,* 18 (1972), 147-161.
36. KINSBOURNE, M. "Looking and Listening Strategies and Beginning Reading," in J.T. Guthrie (Ed.), *Aspects of Reading Instruction.* Baltimore: Johns Hopkins University Press, 1976, 141-161.
37. KOHLBERG, L. "Early Education: A Cognitive-Developmental View," unpublished manuscript, University of Chicago, n.d.
38. KOTTMEYER, W. "Readiness for Reading," *Elementary English,* 24 (October 1947), 355-366.
39. MACGINITIE, W.H. "Evaluating Readiness for Learning to Read: A Critical Review and Evaluation of Research," *Reading Research Quarterly,* 4 (1969), 396-410.
40. MCGRAW, M.B. *Growth: A Study of Johnny and Jimmy.* New York: Appleton-Century-Croft, 1935.
41. MONROE, M. *Children Who Cannot Read.* Chicago: University of Chicago Press, 1936.
42. MOORE, O. "O.K.'s Children," *Time,* November 7, 1960, 103.
43. MORGAN, M.T., and N. ROBINSON. "The 'Back to Basics' Movement in Education," *Canadian Journal of Education,* 1 (1976), 1-11.
44. MORPHETT, M., and C. WASHBURNE. "When Should Children Begin to Read?" *Elementary School Journal,* 31 (March 1931), 496-503.
45. PATRICK, G.T.W. "Should Children under Ten Learn to Read and Write?" *Popular Science Monthly,* January 1899, 382-391.
46. ROBERSON, D.R. "Parents and Teachers: Partners in the Teaching of Reading," *Reading Teacher,* 23 (1970), 722-726.
47. ROBINSON, H.M. *Why Pupils Fail in Reading.* Chicago: University of Chicago Press, 1946.
48. SAMUELS, S.J. "Hierarchical Subskills in Reading Acquisition," in J.T. Guthrie (Ed.), *Aspects of Reading Acquisition.* Baltimore: Johns Hopkins University Press, 1976, 162-179.
49. SHELDON, W.D., and L.W. CARILLO. "Relation of Parents, Home, and Certain Developmental Characteristics to Children's Reading Ability," *Elementary School Journal,* 52 (1952), 262-270.

50. SMITH, F. *Understanding Reading.* New York: Holt, Rinehart and Winston, 1971.
51. SMITH, F. *Psycholinguistics and Reading.* New York: Holt, Rinehart and Winston, 1971.
52. SMITH, N.B. *American Reading Instruction.* Newark, Delaware: International Reading Association, 1965.
53. STRANG, R. "Should Parents Teach Reading?" in W.B. Barbe (Ed.), *Teaching Reading: Selected Materials.* New York: Oxford University Press, 1965, 391-394.
54. SULLIVAN and MCCARTHY. "An Evaluation of Reading Readiness Materials," *Education,* 62 (September 1941), 40-43.
55. TAYLOR, J.E. "Making Sense: The Basic Skill in Reading," *Language Arts,* 54 (1977), 668-672.
56. TRAUB, R., and others. *Openness in Schools: An Evaluation Study.* Toronto: Ontario Institute for Studies in Education, 1976.
57. WARD, E. "A Child's First Reading Teacher: His Parents," *Reading Teacher,* 23 (1970), 756-759.
58. WARTENBURG, H. "Parents in the Reading Program," *Reading Teacher,* 23 (1970), 717-721, 740.
59. YOUNG, N., and E.L. GAIER. "Implications in Emotionally Caused Reading Retardations," *Elementary English,* 28 (1951), 271-275.

Beginning Reading in England

Vera Southgate
University of Manchester
Manchester, England

At IRA's First World Congress on Reading, held in Paris in 1966, the writer presented a paper on beginning reading in England. Since then, a noticeable change in direction has occurred in the views of the public at large, parents, and educators concerning the early stages of teaching reading in England.

Background Features of Infant Education

Three features of the English education system are of particular relevance as a background to the early stages of reading: the length of infant education, the flexibility of the English education system, and the autonomy of the head teacher.

Length of Infant Education

The first stage of compulsory education is the infant stage, from five to seven years. It is followed by the junior stage from seven to eleven years. As most schools accept children into infant classes at the beginning of the term in which they will reach their fifth birthday, many children are only four years, eight months when they begin full-time schooling. Promotions from infant to junior classes take place once a year and depend solely on chronological age, not on educational performance. All children who have reached their seventh birthday during the preceding school year are promoted to junior classes every September. Thus, depending on their dates of birth, different goups of children spend from two years, four months to three years in infant classes. Teachers frequently deplore these variations, pointing out that, in learning to read, "summer born" children are seriously handicapped in comparison with "autumn born" children who spend eight months longer as infants.

Flexibility of Education System

The second important feature is the flexibility of the English education system. Central or local control of what takes place within the schools is minimal. The organisation of classes, the content of the curriculum, the time devoted to various subjects, and the ways of teaching reading vary from school to school at the discretion of the head teacher. This flexibility complicates communication with educationalists from other countries, as it is rather difficult to generalise about practices in English schools. One example will highlight this point. At a national level, the Education Act of 1944 does not even specifically say that children should be taught to read and write. The lack of directive in this matter, however, should not be taken to imply that infant teachers do not regard reading as important. Certainly, the writer does not know of any infant school which fails to incorporate reading into its activities. On the other hand, great variations exist in different schools in the emphasis placed on reading and the ways of teaching it.

The Autonomy of the Head Teacher

The third feature is closely related to the second. Within their own schools, head teachers enjoy almost complete autonomy in matters relating to the education and general welfare of their pupils. Although Her Majesty's Inspectors (representing the government) as well as local advisers and inspectors may offer advice, it would only be in exceptional circumstances that they would issue directives. Neither has it been expected, until recently, that parents should have any say in what is taught or how it should be taught.

Head teachers of schools are quite free to decide on the schools' general approach to teaching reading and the selection of reading materials, money allocated to schools for books and equipment being spent solely at their discretion. In practice, such decisions usually arise from joint discussions between head teacher and staff, so they agree on a general policy about teaching reading. In some schools, however, head teachers encourage their staffs to follow their own ideas about reading, with the result that different methods and materials may be used in different classes in the same school. This freedom to use whatever means they consider appropriate for helping children to learn to read is cherished by English infant teachers.

Organisation and Procedures in Infant Classes

The legal maximum number of infant pupils per class is forty but in practice, with exceptions such as crowded innercity schools, the number is usually nearer thirty pupils. The recent decline in the birth rate has resulted in even smaller classes. While there are a few male infant teachers, most infant teachers are female.

The school day for all infants usually lasts from 9:00 AM to 3:30 PM, with breaks of one and one-half hours for lunch and fifteen minutes in the morning and afternoon.

Infant classes always consist of both boys and girls, and the children are usually of mixed abilities. In the majority of schools, all the children in a class are of the same age and the whole class moves up to a new teacher every year or more frequently. Some schools, however, now use "family" or "vertical" grouping. Then, each class is made up of children with a complete range of chronological ages from under five to over seven. These children probably stay with the same teacher for their entire infant education. There are also variations of total family grouping which include five and six year olds grouped together and seven year olds separated.

Many infant classes have no timetables but work what is known as an "integrated day." Reading and writing activities merge into or are integrated with creative activities, science, or mathematics throughout the day, according to the prevailing interests of the pupils and teacher. Those schools which consider reading as a top priority clearly devote more time to it than schools which emphasize creative activities of all kinds. Certain schools try to achieve a balance by arranging reading, writing, and number activities in the mornings and creative activities in the afternoons. Such flexible patterns of planning result in different schools, or even children in the same school or class, spending varying amounts of time on reading and writing activities.

The regimes in most infant schools are now either "open" or moving in that direction. The whole atmosphere is informal, happy, and busy within colourful and exciting environments. A truly "formal" infant class would be a rarity. It would be quite unusual, for instance, to find infants sitting in rows, facing the front of the classroom. Instead, children sit in small groups and talk to each other about what they are doing. Children generally move about the room or throughout the school informally and there are many opportunities for them to engage in individual pursuits, such as playing with sand and water, painting, constructing models, serving in shops, dressing up and acting, reading, or writing.

Reading in Infant Classes

Despite variations in ways of teaching beginning reading in England, it is possible, by disregarding extremes, to draw a broad picture of common practices in the majority of infant classes.

Infant Reading Schemes

Although basic reading schemes are used fairly extensively, the schemes themselves, and ways of using them, differ from schemes and practices in the United States and Canada. English reading schemes are much smaller, both in size of books and amount of supporting materials. Supporting materials, other than slim supplementary books, are not always purchased. Teachers' manuals are fairly small and their tone is suggestive rather than didactic. Yet, certain schools fail to purchase teachers' manuals; not all teachers read them; and very few faithfully follow the guidelines.

Only a few schools rely solely on one reading scheme and even they tend to use parts of other schemes and additional supplementary books.

The most up-to-date information available about reading practices in infant classes is found in the Bullock Report (5) discussed later in this paper. It reports that, in 1973, only 19 percent of schools attended by six year olds used just one commercial reading scheme; 53 percent used books from several reading schemes, along with other books which the teachers had graded in order of difficulty; and the remaining 28 percent used commercial schemes together with other books, not all of which were graded.

The reading schemes in most common use are vocabulary controlled and they employ a look-and-say method. The Bullock Report, for instance, found that 79 percent of the classes for six year olds used Key Words Reading Scheme and 89 percent used "other vocabulary controlled types of reading schemes." These, no doubt, would include schemes published in the 1950s, e.g. *Janet and John (11)*, *The McKee Readers (8)*, *The Happy Trio Reading Scheme (6)*, and *Happy Venture Readers (13)*. A further 31 percent used *Breakthrough to Literacy (7)*, a "language experience" scheme published in 1970. In fact, in nearly every infant school, one could find parts of the six schemes mentioned as well as many others.

Two recently published schemes are now finding their ways into many schools. *Link Up (12)* is broadly a language experience scheme, with the sentence structure based on the patterns found in the spoken language of urban five and six year olds. While provision is made for some phonic instruction, the main emphasis is on comprehension. In contrast, the vocabulary of *Language in Action (9)* has been chosen to highlight a system of "spelling pattern progression." Each of the first books is designed to teach the sound of a single letter. In later stories, letters are combined by the use of a synthetic phonics method. Later books incorporate increasingly complex grammatical and syntactical patterns.

Reading schemes generally use the medium of t.o. (traditional orthography). Bullock found that only 9.1 percent of classes containing six year olds used i.t.a. (Initial Teaching Alphabet). In the early stages, a further 3.6 percent used schemes employing some form of colour coding.

Teachers' General Practices

The formal teaching of reading and writing does not commence as soon as children start school. Neither is it usual for teachers to adopt formal programmes to develop prereading skills, e.g. visual and auditory discrimination. Instead there is an informal, generalised approach to language skills and an encouragement of their gradual development as a means of communication, first by speaking and listening and later by the introduction of small items of reading and writing.

During the first few terms, teachers read stories to children and share attractive well-illustrated books with small groups. Then, as children pick up books from the book corner and examine all the surrounding display tables, pictures, and models, their interest is fostered in printed and written words. Many of the pictures and activities have clearly printed notices attached. The children soon learn to read these in order to find out the names of objects on the nature table; who has made the intriguing model; or when they, themselves, may paint, serve in the shop, or play in the Wendy house. During this early stage, children probably learn to read and write their own names, perhaps by first putting them on pictures they have painted. Later, they will want to write something underneath their pictures, e.g. "This is my mummy." Their teacher will help them write these words and read what they have written. This stage is generally followed by the children wanting to write small stories, which at first may only be one sentence or two. Such procedures are broadly language experience based.

When the children have developed a small vocabulary of sight words and the teacher considers them sufficiently interested to begin more formal work, a reading scheme based on a look-and-say method will probably be introduced. The names of the characters and the early words in the first book will probably be learned through flash card practice and games, in small group situations. Later, with the teacher's help, the children could examine the first page or two of the book, and so learn to read it.

Once children have begun a reading scheme, an infant teacher's main means of forwarding progress is to "hear" the children read and to prompt them when they fail to recognise a word. As the children in any class are at widely scattered stages in the reading scheme, listening to children reading aloud is done individually or in very small groups. Although very few teachers have begun to look upon errors in oral reading as diagnostic cues, they still regard the practice of hearing children read as the backbone of their reading instruction. The Bullock Committee found that over half the teachers of six year olds heard all the children in their classes read to them at least three or four times a week, the poorer readers receiving more help than the better readers. The teacher generally records the pages each child has read to her on a card kept in the child's book. This is the main, and sometimes the only, system of record keeping in most schools.

Although neither teachers nor pupils in England are acquainted with those "two vowels who go walking," a rule so familiar in U.S. and Canadian classrooms; nevertheless, teachers often do a small amount of incidental phonics training with those children who have made initial progress with a reading scheme. This has generally been analytic phonics work based on words from the children's sight vocabulary. Until recently, however, such work was limited in amount and conception. The 97 percent of infant teachers who reported to the Bullock Committee that they did *some* phonics work in one particular week in 1973, could easily lead people unfamiliar with English infant classes to seriously overestimate the small amount of phonics training which had actually been occurring.

While the teacher is giving attention to an individual child or to groups of children, the rest of the children are likely to be engaged in personal reading, writing, drawing, or other miscellaneous activities. Consequently, the teacher frequently finds herself distracted from listening to a child who is reading aloud to her by children who come to ask for help with spellings, or by others who need encouragement to settle down.

Incidental Reading and Writing

In most infant classes, in addition to some work with a basic reading scheme, there is incidental reading and writing. In every classroom (and frequently in corridors and entrance halls) fiction, poetry, and information books are displayed. Children browse among these books, share them with friends, or examine and read them on their own. In most schools children are allowed to borrow books to take home. The movement toward "progressive" education has also resulted in an enormous surge of written expression from even young children. They write original stories, as well as poetry. They record the interesting events of their days and they engage in miniature "research" among nonfiction books about "projects" on which they are currently working. They then write and illustrate small books on castles or dinosaurs. All this child-initiated reading and writing is continually enriching children's experiences with the written and printed word.

How Important Is the Infant Reading Scheme?

Despite all the other reading and writing going on in their classes, most infant teachers regard a basic reading scheme as the core of their reading teaching, and the selection of the best scheme as vital. The writer, however, has long thought that this rich background of reading and writing was probably responsible for more of young children's reading progress than the work done by teachers in connection with reading schemes. In 1968 she suggested that (14):

> ...the words found in the early stages of a basic reading scheme may represent only a small proportion of the actual printed and written vocabulary with which the child is in contact during his time in school.

A small experiment designed to find out the proportions of time spent on these two different kinds of reading and writing activities was undertaken at Manchester University, and the results were published under the title of "How Important is the Infant Reading Scheme?" (16). Eight classes of five and six year olds in six city schools were selected for the experiment. Each teacher was convinced that her reading teaching was based on her chosen reading scheme. An observation schedule was devised whereby, for periods of 30 minutes, the observer could record at 10 second intervals every reading and writing activity in which a child was engaged. The activities were categorized according to whether they were related to the reading scheme. The results fully confirmed the hypothesis that more time was spent on incidental reading and writing than on the reading scheme. The results showed only slight variations in respect to such variables as age, sex, class, school, or reading scheme.

The simplest way of expressing the results is in terms of a hypothetical hour which the teacher considered to be devoted to reading and writing activities. In such an hour, individual children aged five and six, average in intelligence and verbal activity, spent their time, on average, as follows:

On activities relating to the reading scheme	4 minutes	(7 percent)
On other reading and writing activities	29 minutes	(48 percent)
On extraneous or diversionary activities	27 minutes	(45 percent)

Lest you are startled by the proportion of apparently "wasted" time, the children in all eight classes made average or above average reading progress in the year.

Developments in Reading Philosophies and Practices

The current pattern of teaching beginning reading in England can best be appreciated in the light of developments over the past twenty-five years or so.

Establishment of Look-and-Say Methods

In the prewar years, infant teachers had regarded the teaching of reading as one of their main tasks and phonics as the accepted method of doing so. The period from 1945 onwards, and throughout the 1950s, saw the growth of look-and-say sentence or word methods. Young teachers fresh from college were the chief advocates of such methods, which were frequently looked upon by older teachers as "newfangled nonsense." Nevertheless, new reading schemes published during the 1950s were based on look-and-say methods. Their standard of production, including many coloured illustrations, made them more attractive than the older phonics readers. Schools began to buy and use them and some are still being used (6, 8, 11, 13). Unfortunately, during this time, many teachers grew to accept that the use of the look-and-say methods precluded the need for any phonics teaching.

Growth of Progressive Practices

During the 1950s England also experienced the earliest beginnings of progressive, informal, or open infant schools. The movement increased during the 1960s and the final seal of approval was put on it by the Plowden Report (4) in 1967 (i.e. one year after IRA's Paris Congress). Although only a minority of infant schools (perhaps about 15-20 percent) have ever been run on truly progressive lines, the movement nevertheless affected reading in a number of ways. First, there was the implied suggestion that learning to read was less important than other activities, such as "creative activities." The 500 page *Plowden Report*, which covered all aspects of primary education, devoted only five pages specifically to reading and, of these, only one page to teaching children to read. The assumption began to be accepted that if children were "surrounded by beautiful books" (a phrase frequently used) and were free to handle them, the children would all eventually be eager to learn to read. This emphasis on motivation seemed to imply that motivation would automatically be followed by learning. The teacher was to become a guide and counsellor rather than an instructor. In fact, the word *teaching* became almost a dirty word. It reached the stage that teachers felt called upon to apologise to visitors who might actually find them doing a little direct teaching with a small group of children. Lecturers, also, unless they wished to be regarded as old fashioned, thought it advisable to change their lecture titles from "The Teaching of Reading" to "Children Learning to Read."

Doubts about Progressive Movement

Not everyone was entirely happy about the effects of these progressive regimes on reading and other basic subjects. Teachers in junior schools complained about the lack of reading skills in pupils promoted from infant schools, and remedial reading teachers found their loads increasing. A few reading experts began to suggest that, if all children were to become successful readers, perhaps more was needed than just motivation and general encouragement.

A Personal Viewpoint

In a paper entitled "The Importance of Structure in Beginning Reading" (15), this writer said:

> When emphasis is on learning, the main danger is that the teacher will assume that in a stimulating environment, with freedom to explore and experiment, all children will eventually want to learn to read, and will be able to do so without specific instruction.
>
> ...in infant classes... the freer the atmosphere and the more informal the working procedures, the more imperative it becomes that the reading environment should be so structured, as not only to encourage reading, but also to forward its progress.

In 1969, some people considered these views to be reactionary. In fact, the writer was searching for a balanced programme which would consist of highly motivated learning situations, supported by knowledgeable, carefully planned teaching programmes.

In 1971, a research report (1) was published which lent support to the writer's conclusions. Reporting on twelve infant schools in deprived areas, the authors found that "...initial reading success does not prove to be associated with what are sometimes loosely considered to be 'progessive' methods...." They concluded that the major difference between schools successful and unsuccessful in teaching reading was "the lack of systematic instruction in the unsuccessful schools," in which they noted a considerable neglect of phonics, few set periods of reading instruction, and a delay in beginning to teach reading until children manifested spontaneous interest in it. In contrast, in the successful schools, reading instruction tended to be organised and recognizable from the start, and early phonics instruction was common. The one exception to this general trend was the most successful school of all, in which activity methods and creativity were combined with a certain amount of teacher direction. This last regime is exactly the one which the writer would support.

The Black Papers

Meanwhile, a much more definite reaction against "progressive educational methods" had been fermenting in the minds of nonreading specialists—employers, educational journalists, and others. The reaction erupted in a series of Black Papers. The first two were published in 1969 (*2, 3*) and the fifth appeared in 1977. The authors attributed falling standards in reading, writing, and spelling to progressive methods, lack of formal teaching, and lack of discipline. Firm research evidence was noticeably missing from many of these papers, which relied mostly on anecdotal accounts of reading standards in the authors' younger days. The authors' solutions tended to lie in an advocacy of the theme of returning to the good old days of formal teaching. A great deal of the national press supported the views of the Black Papers. One educational journalist, however, noted that:

> The Black Paper writers seem peculiarly detached from 1975. They belong in a mythical golden age when academic standards were high and all children could read.

However, even apart from the Black Paper writers, general concern about reading standards was increasing. It was intensified in 1972 by the publication of *The Trend of Reading Standards* (*17*), giving the results of the latest national reading survey undertaken by the Department of Education and Science. In contrast to previous surveys undertaken between 1948 and 1964 which had established a trend of successively higher reading standards for eleven and fifteen year olds, this latest survey suggested that average test scores were leveling out or falling behind.

The Bullock Committee

The shock of this report provoked questions in the House of Commons, which resulted in the setting up of a Government Committee of Inquiry into Reading and the Use of English. This committee, chaired by Sir Alan Bullock, was the first government committee ever to have been concerned with reading. Its report, *A Language for Life* (*5*), commonly referred to as the Bullock Report, was published in 1975.

Regarding the formal/progressive controversy, the Bullock Report took a balanced view about midway between the progressives and the formal traditionalists. It viewed the teaching of reading against the broadest possible background of language development in all areas of the curriculum. While lending support to many of the progressive aspects of primary education, it also emphasised the need for some specific teaching in the fields of reading and written expression. For instance, it stated:

> It is unrealistic to expect every child to be a competent reader on leaving the infant school. But the foundation of reading should be firmly laid there and not left until the child reaches the junior school.

The report also indicated that both phonics and spelling should be taught.

In the long run, the publication of the Bullock Report is bound to affect the teaching of beginning reading in England. The idea of the importance of some structure in the teaching of reading is becoming accepted. Teachers who received little initial training in teaching reading are now anxious to increase their expertise. Enrollments are increasing for courses of inservice training and for the Open University's course in Reading Development. Thus, the number of teachers knowledgeable in the field of reading is growing considerably.

Education—The Great Debate

In 1977, public concern about standards of literacy and numeracy was becoming vociferous. Employers, parents, and educationists were expressing themselves with great firmness; and banner headlines in the press about falling standards were almost daily occurrences. The furor had been partly sparked by grave economic problems: the public wanted to see results for all the money being spent on education. The Prime Minister agreed that the question of "Standards" would be looked into. National surveys and enquiries were set up and the Secretary of State for Education held a series of regional meetings entitled "Education—The Great Debate." Discussions were concentrated on the establishment of a core curriculum and more effective methods of monitoring progress. The results are clearly going to be that, in the future, industrialists and parents will demand higher standards in reading and in written work and will expect more say in what is done in schools.

Looking to the Future

Current concerns with educational standards and practices, which are strongly declared as those outlined, cannot fail to influence future educational practices, including beginning reading. The writer suspects that the following changes may well occur:

1. Infant teachers will give higher priority to the teaching of reading.
2. Teachers are likely to incorporate more formal teaching into their progressive or open regimes.
3. The teaching of phonics will become part of planned reading programmes.
4. There will be more assessment, diagnosis, and record keeping than has been usual in infant classes.
5. There will be a greater emphasis on encouraging children to be task-oriented.
6. Children will be expected to put more effort into learning to read.
7. Parents will expect to have some say in what and how their children are taught and some will want to help with reading in schools (a few already do).

The writer hopes that changes will be forward looking rather than representing a nostalgic return to older methods. She would like to see changes directed toward the achievement of a balance between children who are strongly motivated to learn to read and teachers who are not only eager to encourage them but are also prepared to engage in specific and knowledgeable teaching at appropriate points.

The question one would then be asking would not be whether reading standards were rising or falling, but whether the children were progressing at their optimum rate—a more difficult but more worthwhile question. The writer's belief is that highly motivated and knowledgeable teachers of reading could so inspire and support children in their learning, as to ensure that *all* children would learn to read faster and would progress further than teachers have previously imagined possible.

References

1. CANE, B., and J. SMITHERS. *The Roots of Reading.* Slough: National Foundation for Educational Research, 1971.
2. COX, C.B., and A.E. DYSON. (Eds.). "Fight for Education: A Black Paper," *The Critical Quarterly Society,* 1969 (2 Radcliffe Avenue, London N.W. 10).
3. COX, C.B., and A.E. DYSON (Eds.). "Black Paper Two: The Crisis in Education," *The Critical Quarterly Society,* 1969.
4. DEPARTMENT OF EDUCATION AND SCIENCE. *Children in Their Primary Schools* (The Plowden Report). London: Her Majesty's Stationery Office, 1967.
5. DEPARTMENT OF EDUCATION AND SCIENCE. *A Language for Life* (The Bullock Report). London: Her Majesty's Stationery Office, 1975.
6. GRAY, W.S., and others. *The Happy Trio Reading Scheme.* Exeter: Wheaton, 1956.
7. MacKAY, D., and B. THOMPSON. *Breakthrough to Literacy.* London: Longman, 1970.
8. McKEE, P., and others. *The McKee Readers.* London: Nelson, 1956.
9. MORRISS, J.M. *Language in Action.* Basingstoke: Macmillan, 1974.
10. MURRAY, W. *Key Words Reading Scheme.* Loughborough: Wills and Hepworth, 1964.
11. O'DONNELL, M., and R. MUNRO. *Janet and John.* Welwyn: Nisbet, 1949.
12. REID, J., and J. LOW. *Link Up.* Edinburgh: Holmes McDougall, 1973.
13. SCHONELL, F.J. *The Happy Venture Readers.* Edinburgh: Oliver and Boyd, 1958.
14. SOUTHGATE, V. "Formulae for Beginning Reading Tuition," *Educational Research,* 11, 23-30.
15. SOUTHGATE, V. "The Importance of Structure in Beginning Reading," in K. Gardner (Ed.), *Reading Skills: Theory and Practice.* London: Ward Lock Educational, 1970.
16. SOUTHGATE, V., and C.Y. LEWIS. "How Important Is the Infant Reading Scheme?" *Reading,* 7 (1973).
17. START, K.B., and B.K. WELLS. *The Trend of Reading Standards.* Slough: National Foundation for Educational Research, 1972.

Public Primary Reading Instruction in Mexico

Robert Miller
East Side Union High School District
Los Gatos, California
United States of America

Over 7.2 million people of Mexican origin who are concentrated in the southwestern portion of the United States and approximately 3,000 illegal immigrants who enter the United States each night present a major challenge to the educational system of America (*4*). Of this number, 1.6 million Spanish speakers make metropolitan Los Angeles one of the world's largest Spanish speaking cities. Even though there are so many Mexicans in the United States, there is very little information available on the components of the Mexican educational system, especially the method of teaching reading and language arts. This information is important for correctly placing students and for determining the expectations of Mexican parents in terms of the school system.

The purpose of this paper is to present a general overview of the Mexican public educational system and to describe the reading and language arts program used in grades one to six as presented in the official documents of the Secretaría de Educación Pública (the Ministry of Public Education).

The Mexican Educational System

The concept of universal education for the people of Mexico was not practiced until 1921. Prior to 1856, the Catholic

Church ran most of the schools with the exception of a few schools based on the teachings of Lancaster. In 1856, under the presidency of Benito Juarez, the federal government took over the schools and education became a function of the state. The Catholic Church continued to run the schools, however, and the status quo was maintained. The official statistics for 1910 indicated that 1) more than two-thirds of the total 1910 population could neither read nor write, 2) fewer than one-fourth of the school age population were enrolled in school, and 3) education in the rural areas was almost completely neglected (*12*).

The federal education movement began in 1921. Many anti-illiteracy campaigns were inaugurated in the 1920s, 1930s, and 1940s. From 1946-1952, 5,069 new primary schools were added to the 12,000 already in existence. As of the 1976-1977 school year, there were 53,571 primary schools with an enrollment of 12,148,221 students and the literacy rate was approximately 80 percent of the population (*13*).

Mexican education is highly centralized with all plans and programs, textbooks, and curriculum materials being written and approved by the Ministry of Public Education. The Secretario de Educación Pública is assisted by five sub-secretaries, each with several departments under his authority. In terms of budget, this organizationl structure for 1978-1979 cost more than the equivalent of thirty-one million American dollars with primary school instruction consuming approximately 33 percent of the total (*2*). Primary education is under the direction of the Secretario de Educación Básica and has two divisions for primary education: primary education in Mexico City and primary education in the states. The directors of the four divisions are under the director of primary education in Mexico City. These divisions are geographic and are designed to make easier the administration of the 2,444 schools in Mexico City. Each division is further divided into zones and there are inspectors who supervise the implementation of the official curriculum.

The schools are administered by a director who is responsible for dealing with parents, the central office, and public relations. Day-to-day operation of the school is handled by a secretary who is a certified teacher. Schools usually have six grades and are divided into sections. School starts at either 8:00 a.m. or 2:00 p.m. and lasts until 12:30 or 6:30 p.m. Students attend only one shift, but teachers often teach for two shifts. The students are taught language, mathematics, natural science, social science, technical education, art, and physical education.

Teachers are appointed and have tenure from the time they are first hired. They can be removed only through resignation, abandonment of employment, mental health, physical disability, or death. Teachers are paid a base salary plus a cost of living adjustment, depending upon where they live. In order to be a teacher, candidates must have completed six years of elementary school and three years of secondary school. Next, candidates spend three years in normal school and take the state examinations in the fourth year.

Textbooks are provided free to all students. They are developed and printed in Mexico City and all teachers are required to use them. In addition to the textbooks, each teacher receives the *Plan y Programas* book which lists all of the objectives plus activities for the objectives. Teachers also receive a *Teacher's Manual* which explains the rationale for each activity.

Reading Instruction in Mexico

In the first grade Teacher's Manual for the Mexican primary schools, there is a criticism for each of the standard methods of reading instruction (phonetic, global, and eclectic). According to the manual, the phonetic approach produces a situation whereby the students do not understand what is read (1). The global method is criticized because it makes little use of the sounds of Spanish which are relatively regular in terms of pronunciation, spelling, and writing. The eclectic method is criticized because there is not a synthesis between the phonetic and global elements, i.e., they remain as distinct entities. Mexican educators are currently using a system called "methodo global de análisis estructural" which combines the global system, structural analysis, and continuous associations including speaking, writing, and reading the same words. All of the textbooks in all subject areas have been written to reflect this system. For example, in reading, sight words are taught first and, in math, models are used to present the total concept. After the whole is presented, the component parts are studied.

Before discussing the actual curriculum, it would be prudent to consider the relationship between reading and writing in Spanish. It is generally believed that Spanish possesses one of the highest correlations between the spoken sound and the written symbol (3). There are twenty-nine letters and twenty-four spoken units. The implications of this regular grapheme-phoneme relationship are important. This may be the reason that little time is spent on teaching spelling and the vocabulary and content of the textbooks are not controlled by a graded word list as is found in basal readers used in the United States.

In the official curriculum, reading is an integral part of language study. Modiano (5) summarized the program used prior to 1972:

> The federal and state language curriculum is outlined in the federal textbooks, workbooks, and instructional manuals. The first year of school includes an introduction to reading, primarily phonic in approach, beginning with the mastery of vowel sounds, then consonants, blends, the order of presentation from easiest to most difficult. By the end of the first year students are expected to know the entire alphabet and be able to read by sounding out words. They should also be able to form all letters in cursive script, to know the use of capitals and small letters, also punctuation marks such as periods, question marks, and exclamation points and to understand some simple grammatical rules dealing with gender and other suffix changes.
>
> In the second year, silent reading is introduced as is reading comprehension and the interpretation of written material. Handwriting should be improved, the student should be able to take simple dictation, free composition is begun, previous work is reviewed, and more grammatical rules are included. There is a review of the semi-irregular letters in Spanish orthography, accents, and more punctuation marks.

In 1972, the entire curriculum was revised. Commissions were established and new plan books, teacher's manuals, and textbooks were printed. The plan books (*Plan y Programas de Estudio para la Educación Primaria*) are written for each of the six grades and contain objectives and activities for each month of the school year. The objectives and activities are referenced to pages in the textbooks, teacher's manuals, and student workbooks. In the case of physical education and arts and crafts, there are descriptions of the activities to be accomplished. The teacher's books detail the exact procedure to be used and justify the reasons for using the procedure. Textbooks are the property of the students and are provided without cost to students in both public and private schools.

First Grade

There are three parts to the system of teaching reading: 1) preparation, 2) learning to read and write, and 3) consolidating the gains.

The vast majority of students enter first grade at age six years without preschool or readiness training (*8*). During the first months of the first grade, reading readiness is taught and students work on body coordination, distinguishing objects by size and shape, observation, hand-eye coordination, tracing letters, and developing the ability to describe things. They also learn muscle control and perceptual activities. Also, during the first month, the students are expected to learn the colors: red, green, yellow, blue, black, and white. A typical lesson would be for the teacher to write the following on the blackboard:

el es rojo. (The shoe is red.)

la es roja. (The window is red.)

After the teacher writes this, the students copy the examples in their notebooks. Individual students are then asked to read from the board. Successful answers are rewarded either by teacher acknowledgment or by applause from the other students in the class. This type of assignment normally takes about thirty minutes.

During the second month, the students continue with readiness activities and learn the parts of the body and the parts of the face. Each phoneme is also learned, but it is learned as a part of a syllable rather than in isolation.

The students trace letters, work on oral skills, and learn the names of animals during the third month. Oral activities are emphasized. Students are required to tell about a dialogue, memorize brief selections, or tell about a picture.

In the fourth and fifth months, the students continue to learn the phonemes, consonants, vowels, and syllables. The remainder of the first grade deals with practicing the rest of the letters, doing oral comprehension, and reading short stories. By the end of first grade, students are expected to know how to read.

Students are also taught how to print the letters. Since 1972, cursive writing has not been taught in the public schools. This means that students graduating from Mexican public schools can only print.

The first grade objectives are accomplished through two books, both of which contain many pictures and are in color. The first book contains pictures which the students color or cut out and paste in a different part of the book (*Libro Recortalbe*) and the second book contains poems, stories, and short biographies of famous Mexican leaders. Both books are referenced to the objectives in the *Plans and Programs* book (*6*).

Second Grade

In the second grade, readiness activities are continued. Students trace letter combinations and work on visual discrimination, two syllable words, and the difficult phonemes and blends such as /z/, /s/, /c/, /gu/, /k/, /y/, and /h/. The graphemes /ll/, /y/, /b/, and /v/ are studied. At this level, students learn the names of the letters.

Comprehension is introduced in several different ways. In some classes the students are required to write a dictation each day. Questions are then asked about the dictation. In other classes, students read stories and then answer the questions. Paramount is oral comprehension and fluency; thus, the students are expected to note punctuation when reading orally, do choral poetry, and paraphrase written selections. Questions are asked by the teacher with the intent of teaching inferences, cause, sequence, and principal ideas. It is important to note that students are expected to find the principal ideas in the entire selection rather than the main idea in each paragraph. From the observations and discussions with teachers, it seems that oral fluency is more important than comprehension. In addition to the above, language skills such as periods, question marks, nouns, subjects, predicates, and adjectives are introduced (7).

Third Grade

Third grade is the year when advanced skills are introduced. Reading readiness activities focus on sophisticated observation and description exercises, classification, sequence, and oral description of what is observed. Comprehension and study skills are stressed during this year. Skills such as endings for stories, main ideas in paragraphs, summaries, comparison of stories, identification of main characters, interpretation of proverbs, and best titles are stressed as well as reading instructions, locating dates in magazines, dictionary skills, newspapers, alphabetical order, sequence, and the use of encyclopedias.

Types of sentences and proper punctuation are stressed in the grammar portion of the course. In addition, the parts of speech and agreement are taught. In two of the classrooms visited, the teachers were working on the types of sentences. The exercises consisted of writing in the notebooks and answering questions from the teacher. Dictation and board work also played important parts in the classrooms visited.

Oral activities are very important during the third grade. Students are again expected to read fluently, describe errors in drawings, summarize stories, tell experiences, do reports, use dramatics to perfect oral language, and understand oral directions. The oral reading stress is on pronouncing phonemes that do not have a high sound symbol correlation. Examples are: /m/ after /pr/, and /rr/, /b/ and /v/, /y/ and /ll/, and /c/ and /q/ (8).

Fourth Grade

In the fourth grade, the oral reading objectives are cut in half and language skills objectives are more than doubled. Oral work consists of narrating stories, description, techniques of interviews, and rhyming. On the other hand, the language objectives consist of the parts of speech, the nominal construction, transformation of nouns, plurals, accents, conjunctions, and tense. In addition to the above, the students are expected to know the difference between fiction and nonfiction.

Study skills taught are parts of a book, diagrams, newspapers, magazines, dictionary skills, maps, logical relationships, bibliographies, and logical operations.

Comprehension skills include reading complete stories, finding the main character, main ideas, central theme, secondary characters, cause-effect, and context clues (9).

Fifth Grade

In the fifth grade, language skills are reduced and study skills are increased. The students are expected to work with popular materials; edit themes; know the nominal construction; utilize conjunctions and prepositions; know the difference between descriptive and narrative; develop rhymes; know several forms of objects and modifiers; do letter writing; and study verbs, adverbs, and tense. In addition, the students do reports on sports and work on rhyming.

Under the heading of study skills, the students are expected to learn how to take notes and how to use encyclopedias, newspapers, graphs, plans, thermometers, and maps. The concept of logical relationships is also studied. Each year some of the same concepts are taught, but they become increasingly more difficult.

The concept of analogy is taught as well as the pronunciation of the following graphemes: b and v, que, gui, and gue. Students are expected to locate stressed syllables and know morphemes. Comprehension skills consist of summarizing, principal ideas, interpretation of prose, and poetry (10).

Sixth Grade

In the sixth grade, language skills are the most important. The student is expected to master the subject, predicate, nominal construction, capital letter rules, direct and indirect objects, tense accent, comma rules, style, and the demonstrative pronouns.

Comprehension skills are focused on relationships with analogies, logical summaries, interpreting illustrations, and main ideas. Study skills complement the study of comprehension because the students are required to learn organizing and recording information. Dictionaries, phone directories, and map reading are mastered. The vocabulary and oral work center on refinement of the language. The students are expected to learn figurative language, homonyms, scientific language, synonyms, and metaphors. They are also expected to read to an audience; comment on stories in the text; do narratives; and react to stories, prose, and verse (11).

Summary

The Mexican educational system is highly centralized with all plans, programs, textbooks, curriculum materials, and teacher training programs controlled by the Ministry of Education. Each teacher is required to follow a set program and enforcement is assured through a corps of inspectors responsible for the schools.

The official method of reading instruction is the "metodo global de análisis estructural" which is translated as the global method with structural analysis. First grade students are taught the sight words for the colors, parts of the face and body, drinks, fruits, and common animals. Word parts are taught and, by the end of the first grade, the student can read with oral fluency. Second grade skills include inferences, cause, sequence, and principal ideas in the total selection. Study skills using dictionaries, newspapers, encyclopedias, and alphabetical order are introduced in the third grade. Grammar is the main concern of the fourth grade, as well as advanced comprehension and study skills. Fifth grade skills focus on interpretation of prose and poetry, analogies, grammar, and study skills. In the sixth grade, vocabulary and oral work center on refinement of the language. Students are expected to learn figurative language, scientific language, and metaphors. They are expected to read to an audience; comment on stories in the text; and react to stories, prose, and verse.

References

1. *Español—Primer Grado*. Mexico: Secretaría de Educación Pública, 1978.
2. *Estadística Básica del Sistema Educativo Nacional. Dirección General de Programación de la Secretaría de Educación Pública Ciclo Escolar 1976-77*. Mexico: Secretaría de Educación Pública, 1978.

3. GRAY, WILLIAM. *The Teaching of Reading and Writing*. Paris: Unesco, 1956.
4. "It's Your Turn in the Sun," *Time*, October 16, 1978, 12.
5. MODIANO, NANCY. "Reading Comprehension in the National Language: A Comparative Study of Bilingual and All Spanish Approaches to Reading Instruction in Selected Indian Schools in the Highlands of Chiapas, Mexico," doctoral dissertation, New York University, 1966.
6. *Plan y Programas de Estudio para la Educación Primaria. Primer Grado.* Mexico: Secretaría de Educación Pública, 1977.
7. *Plan y Programas de Estudio para la Educación Primaria. Segundo Grado.* Mexico: Secretaría de Educación Pública, 1977.
8. *Plan y Programas de Estudio para la Educación Primaria. Tercero Grado.* Mexico: Secretaría de Educación Pública, 1977.
9. *Plan y Programas de Estudio para la Educación Primaria. Cuarto Grado.* Mexico: Secretaría de Educación Pública, 1977.
10. *Plan y Programas de Estudio para la Educación Primaria. Quinto Grado.* Mexico: Secretaría de Educación Pública, 1977.
11. *Plan y Programas de Estudio para la Educación Primaria. Sexto Grado.* Mexico: Secretaría de Educación Pública, 1977.
12. Justo Sierra. *La Educación Nacional.* Mexico: Universidad Nacional Autonoma de Mexico, 1948.
13. *Sistema Educativo Nacional Prontuario Estadístico 1970-79.* Mexico: Secretaría de Educación Pública, July 1978.